D1426116

More
HIGH
SCHOOL
GRADUATES

More
HIGH SCHOOL GRADUATES

How Schools Can Save Students From **Dropping Out**

BEN LEVIN

Foreword by **Michael Fullan**

A Joint Publication

CORWIN
A SAGE Company

FOR INFORMATION:

Corwin

A SAGE Company

2455 Teller Road

Thousand Oaks, California 91320

(800) 233-9936

Fax: (800) 417-2466

www.corwin.com

SAGE Ltd.

1 Oliver's Yard

55 City Road

London, EC1Y 1SP

United Kingdom

SAGE India Pvt. Ltd.

B 1/I 1 Mohan Cooperative Industrial Area

Mathura Road, New Delhi

India 110 044

SAGE Asia-Pacific Pte. Ltd.

33 Pekin Street #02-01

Far East Square

Singapore 048763

Acquisitions Editor: Arnis Burvikovs

Associate Editor: Desirée A. Bartlett

Editorial Assistant: Kimberly Greenberg

Production Editor: Cassandra Margaret Seibel

Copy Editor: Erin Livingston

Typesetter: Hurix Systems Pvt. Ltd.

Proofreader: Susan Schon

Indexer: Jean Casalegno

Cover Designer: Michael Dubowe

Permissions Editor: Karen Ehrmann

Copyright © 2012 by Corwin

All rights reserved. When forms and sample documents are included, their use is authorized only by educators, local school sites, and/or noncommercial or nonprofit entities that have purchased the book. Except for that usage, no part of this book may be reproduced or utilized in any form or by any means, electronic or mechanical, including photocopying, recording, or by any information storage and retrieval system, without permission in writing from the publisher.

Printed in the United States of America.

Library of Congress Cataloging-in-Publication Data

Levin, Benjamin.

More high school graduates : how schools can save students from dropping out / Benjamin Levin.

p. cm.

Includes bibliographical references and index.

ISBN 978-1-4129-9224-4 (pbk.)

1. Education, Secondary. 2. Education, Secondary—Aims and objectives. 3. Educational change. 4. High school graduates. 5. Academic achievement. I. Title.

LB1607.L49 2012

373.12'07—dc23

2011036192

Certified Chain of Custody
Promoting Sustainable Forestry
www.sfiprogram.org
SFI-01268

SFI label applies to text stock

11 12 13 14 15 10 9 8 7 6 5 4 3 2 1

Contents

Foreword

By Michael Fullan
Professor Emeritus, Ontario Institute for Studies in Education/
University of Toronto

Ben Levin knows more about how to improve high schools on a very large scale than anyone I know—because he has done it, thought about it, and done more. Best of all, his solution is not arcane and does not cost a lot of money.

Billions of dollars have been spent in the United States over the past 20 years to improve high schools, to no avail. The Gates Foundation bankrolled hundreds of experiments to produce small high schools with an emphasis on establishing learning communities. Ultimately, they declared failure and went on to something else. Chicago Public Schools attacked school improvement diligently since 1988 and were able to show good improvement in many elementary schools, but the lack of progress in high schools was not even worth writing about. In the meantime, high school dropout rates in the United States have been stuck at about a third of the students on the average, and over half for disadvantaged groups. President Obama has set an ambitious target of "becoming number one in the world again (as they were in 1980) in college graduation by 2020." The problem is that nobody knows how to get there. Enter Ben Levin.

In this book , he does not back away from the problem. He first lays out the challenges, not pulling any punches. We need not only to aim high but also to have a plan to accomplish the highest aspirations. He identifies the gobs of money wasted on the wrong solutions, looks closely at why students don't graduate, and examines why it is so hard to change high schools (their size, how leadership must differ in high schools, their subject centeredness, great diversity of student progress, tracking and streaming, and a romantic view that individualism should carry the day).

After building on his experience, from being a precocious student leader and young school trustee some 40 years ago and through his academic career and two stints as deputy minister of education in two provinces, he has learned a great deal. He was able to help put this all together as deputy minister in Ontario from 2004 to 2007. Ontario, with its almost 900 public high schools, has been an unequivocal success story, moving from a flatlined graduation rate of 68% to its present 81% rate and still climbing. With his academic hat on, he made sure that research and learning were built into these efforts, and he has continued to study the wider research on high schools.

He distills what he has learned into four understandable and powerful pillars:

1. Know the status and progress of every student, and the reasons therein.

2. Provide a program that enables all students to achieve a good outcome.

3. Improve daily teaching and learning through specific, focused strategies.

4. Connect schools deeply to their local and broader communities.

Nothing fancy, dramatic, complex, costly, or requiring super-heroic principals or teachers in this mix. You have to read the chapters to get the details, but they are there in chapter and verse, and they are memorable and usable. Our work on whole-system reform is characterized by focus, precision, specificity, partnership, evidence-based results, and of course, "whole systemness." We have written about it before (Levin, 2008; Fullan 2010a, 2010b), but until now nobody has captured in detail the high school reform part of it.

This work and this book are highly accessible. It is what (borrowing a term from Jeff Kluger) I have called "simplexity"—easy to grasp (the simple part), but difficult to put into practice (the complex part). Within Levin's easy-to-say but hard-to-do strategy are the following components:

A plan (focused, specific, and concise)

Infrastructure and resources

Structures, systems, and processes

Dealing with resistance

Indicators of progress

Communicate often and openly

Dealing with distractions

Levin again provides the examples and meaning of putting these elements together. Above all, *More High School Graduates* furnishes both the vision and the strategies to realize it. You would be surprised how many documents on high school reform contain only the broad vision without any means of enacting it. The latter is in Levin's wheelhouse. Levin gives us hope that the big agenda of high school improvement on a very large scale within a short time period (five to seven years) is realistic if we only apply ourselves in the right way. He even gives us the 20-minute-a-day solution, which you can use tomorrow (but make sure it is buttressed by attention to the four pillars).

Get to action now on the pillars—in your own community but also state- and countrywide. Pay attention to the benchmarking performance of top-performing countries in the Programme for International Student Assessment/Organisation for Economic Co-operation and Development (PISA/OECD) such as Finland, Singapore, Canada. Levin has given us the insights and strategies to compete well in both the small local picture and in the larger national and international scene. *More High School Graduates*— read it and reap!

Preface

This book is about the practical steps that can be taken to have more students graduate from high school.

Many proposals have been made over the years and many projects implemented to get better high schools with better graduation rates. Some of these are about new models of high schools, while others propose specific changes in existing schools. What we have not seen very much of, however, is consistent improvement in results across a large number of schools and students.

This book is about how to get those better results, how to see more of your students walk across that stage at graduation with an earned diploma in their hands and a brighter future ahead of them. It is neither a general argument for what schools should look like nor a proposal for a specific program model. Instead, it provides many specific ideas and connects them to an overall strategy and set of priorities.

This book is directed to educators in our high schools—teachers, principals, superintendents, school board members, and those involved with education policy at the state, provincial, or national level. It is intended to inspire but also to guide the kinds of changes you will make to benefit our young people.

Several things set this book apart from the other literature mentioned. First, there is no other book that provides a comprehensive guide to improving all high schools in a district, state, or country. Most of what is written either criticizes high schools as they are now or proposes a particular model for high schools. This book lays out four themes that, taken together, provide a clear road map for improvement.

Second, this book is not based on what I think or hope or believe will work. It is based on what has demonstrably worked. The province of Ontario, Canada, where the ideas in this book were developed and tested, increased its high school graduation rate from 68% in 2004 to 81% in 2010. Across our 900 or so high schools, 18,000 more students are now graduating each year than were seven years ago. Moreover, these practices are now deeply embedded in most Ontario high schools, with strong support from educators. These ideas have been successful in diverse communities and schools, small and large, urban and rural.

Third, the book contains many practical and specific suggestions that can be adopted in any school. They do not require superhuman teachers or principals. They are grounded in an overall strategy and priorities, but they are adaptable to different settings and can be implemented in many different ways. Readers do not have to do or like everything in these pages, but I am confident you will like and want to do many of the things you find here.

Helping our young people get a good education that builds their skills and confidence for life is a huge challenge, but also an enormous opportunity—indeed, a privilege. So many of those working in secondary schools are exceptional people providing exceptional service to students and communities. I hope this book helps you do that work even better.

Acknowledgments

I started my career in education as a high school student leader. In 1968 and 1969, I was vice-president and then president of the student council of West Kildonan Collegiate in Winnipeg, Canada. West Kildonan was a very diverse school in terms of ethnicity and social class, if not color. I was prompted to run because I did not find high school to be a very interesting place intellectually and found it to be highly restrictive in terms of acceptable behavior. I was elected student council president on a "student rights" program. In my senior year, I was also one of the leaders of an effort to create a citywide high school students' union in Winnipeg. That was the genesis of a career in education that now extends over more than 40 years. Although the union never really got established, the experience led me to run for—and be elected to—the board of the Seven Oaks School Division and then to pursue graduate work in education. My career has included several stints as an academic, mainly at The University of Manitoba as well as more than a dozen years as a senior manager of education in government, including three years as deputy minister (chief civil servant) in Manitoba, and later, three years in the same role in a much larger province: Ontario.

In a career that long, one is inevitably influenced by many, many friends and colleagues around the world. My time working with the Canadian Education Association's project on "exemplary high schools," with the Western Research Network on Education and Training, and with the Manitoba School Improvement Program were all important in influencing my thinking about high schools. Among the many people who have shaped the ideas reflected in this book, I must mention Mel Ainscow, Larry Bremner, Ed Buller, Peter Coleman, Amanda Cooper, Amanda Datnow, Ron Duhamel, Lorna Earl, Gerald Farthing, Michael

Fullan, Jane Gaskell, the late Don Girard, Norton Grubb, Andy Hargreaves, Nancy Hoffman, David Hopkins, Heather Hunter, the late Bill Lambie, Linda Lee, Leo LeTourneau, Allan Luke, Penny Milton, Steve Munby, Glenn Nicholls, Susan Nolen, Sharon Pekrul, Clyde Perry, Pat Rowantree, Pasi Sahlberg, Mel West, John Wiens, and the late Maxine Zimmerman.

My time as deputy minister of education in Ontario provided a lab to test many of the ideas in this book. Among the key people in helping Ontario raise its graduation rate so dramatically in the last few years were Premier Dalton McGuinty, Ministers Gerard Kennedy and Kathleen Wynne, and many on the ministry team, including Carol Campbell, Grant Clarke, Dominic Giroux, Aryeh Gitterman, Avis Glaze, Nancy Naylor, Kirsten Parker, Katie Telford, and George Zegarac. A very large number of people in schools and districts across Ontario did important and admirable work.

Some of the research for this book was supported by funds from the Canada Research Chairs Program of the Government of Canada and from a research grant from the Higher Education Quality Council of Ontario. Ontario Institute for Studies in Education (OISE) graduate students Nathalie Carrier, Sachin Maharaj, and Lauren Segedin provided excellent research assistance and contributed to many of the ideas in this book.

Huge thanks, and much more than that, to my wonderful wife, Barbara, who puts up with my endless hours on the computer doing this work.

I would like to dedicate this book to the many outstanding educators who, over the years, have worked to create high schools that value, support, challenge, and stimulate young people. I want to especially mention two colleagues and friends as examples: Brian O'Leary and Jonathan Young, whose sensitivity to and optimism about education and young people have been put into practice over their entire careers in ways that should inspire us all and that have inspired me.

Of course, all interpretations, errors, and omissions are mine alone.

PUBLISHER'S ACKNOWLEDGMENTS

Corwin would like to thank the following individuals for taking the time to provide their editorial insight and guidance:

Virginia E. Kelsen, Assistant Principal
Rancho Cucamonga High School
Rancho Cucamonga, CA

Belinda J. Raines, High School Principal
Northwestern High School
Detroit, MI

John Rice, Director of Science, Technology Education, Health Education, Family and Consumer Sciences, and Health Services
North Syracuse Central School District
North Syracuse, NY

Kelly VanLaeken, Principal
Ruben A. Cirillo High School
Walworth, NY

About the Author

 **Ben Levin** is a professor and Canada Research Chair in Education Leadership and Policy at the Ontario Institute for Studies in Education, University of Toronto. His career is about half as an academic and half as a senior civil servant. He is a graduate of the University of Manitoba, Harvard University, and the University of Toronto, and also holds an honorary degree from the University of Ottawa. He has worked with private research organizations, school districts, provincial governments, and national and international agencies, and built an outstanding academic and research career. As a civil servant, he served as deputy minister (chief civil servant) for education for the province of Ontario from 2004 through 2007, and again from 2008 through 2009. From 1999 through 2002, he was deputy minister of education and of advanced education for the province of Manitoba. As a scholar, he has published seven books and more than 200 other articles on education in professional and academic publications. He gives talks and consults on education issues around the world. His current interests are large-scale change, poverty and inequity, and finding better ways to connect research to policy and practice in education. More information is available at http://webspace.oise.utoronto.ca/~levinben/

CHAPTER ONE

The Challenge

In 2003, education in Ontario, Canada, a province of some 13 million people and 2 million students in nearly 5,000 schools, had experienced 10 years of difficult times. A new high school curriculum and testing system had been introduced. There had been much conflict between the government and the teaching profession, with frequent legislative changes to important aspects of the education system from governance to funding to teacher regulation. Relationships were acrimonious on all sides; many teachers withdrew from extracurricular activities, and private school enrollment increased as students and parents grew frustrated with the difficulties. Worst of all, student outcomes were stagnant or declining. Several reports showed that high school graduation rates in the new four-year high school program were falling, with only 60% of students graduating on time and only 68% of students graduating even after an extra year.

Seven years later, the situation was quite different. By 2010, Ontario's four-year graduation rate had risen to 73% "on time" and 81% after a fifth year. In a system of more than 800 high schools and about 140,000 students in each grade, this meant some 18,000 more graduates each year, and the rate is still increasing. Ontario has moved from being near the bottom among Canadian provinces in graduation rate to being among the best.

Across the world, failure remains an endemic part of secondary education. The most recent figures from the Organisation for Economic Co-operation and Development (OECD), which includes most of the world's large economies, show that in almost all developed countries, 10% or more of their students fail

1

to complete high school at all, and in most countries, the figure is 20% or more. The latest U.S. data show a graduation rate of about 72% (Swanson, 2011), but that percentage is significantly lower among Latinos, African Americans, and Native Americans. These numbers do not include students who require one or more additional years to graduate; nor are those failures evenly distributed. The failure to graduate occurs disproportionately for students growing up in poverty or students from minority groups, but the costs in lost potential, disillusion, and blighted lives are borne by the whole society (Levin, 2009).

Since lower levels of education among parents are strongly associated with lower levels of success in children, the effect is also multigenerational. A recent report by McKinsey (McKinsey & Company, 2009) estimated the cost to the economy of achievement gaps in U.S. schools at $300 billion to $700 billion, or 3% to 5% of gross domestic product (GDP). And people are not happy about the situation either. A 2010 U.S. poll (Alliance for Excellent Education, 2010) found that just one in four of the adults polled gave high schools a good or excellent rating, while 42% gave them a C, and one in five gave them a poor or failing grade. Two-thirds of those polled said that the high school dropout rate has a significant impact on the nation's economy and on America's ability to compete globally.

This book is about how schools and school systems can increase the proportion of students who successfully complete secondary school. Over the last few decades, much has been learned about how to improve individual schools, and there has been some success in improving elementary school outcomes across entire systems. However, improving secondary schools has proved a greater challenge. High schools have features, discussed a little later, that make them very different from elementary schools—and harder to change. There are fewer models of successful change at a system level in secondary schools. Although many proposals have been made for improving high schools, few of them have shown the desired impact.

This book takes the view that we do know how to increase graduation rates in our high schools. It lays out a four-element approach that could be implemented in a school, a district, or a nation. Very little in these pages is new; everything proposed here is being done or has been done in a school or district somewhere. What is different here is bringing together all the key elements in a single overall strategy, with a strong and persistent focus on implementation. Too often, improvement efforts have relied on doing just one thing—a new timetable, a new teaching strategy, or a new teacher advisor system. Each of these has its place, but success depends not on one or two exciting ideas, but on tackling all the vital factors simultaneously and persistently.

The strategy in this book rests on three fundamental beliefs:

First, all high schools need to work on improvement.

Second, improvement cannot come from any single strategy; it requires addressing many aspects of the school's work together and in an integrated way.

Third, improvement is more a matter of sustained effort over time than it is of brilliant design or policy.

These beliefs inform everything else.

A NOTE ON DROPOUTS

This book does not use the term *dropout*. Instead, it talks about high school graduates. One reason for this choice is that it is relatively easy to know who has graduated but much harder to know who is a dropout. More important, the term *dropout* suggests that the failure to complete high school is a choice by a student, whereas the starting point for this book is that all students want to graduate and their failure to do so is virtually always a result of a failed relationship between the student and the school.

In making this claim, I am certainly not blaming schools for every student who does not graduate. Some students bring huge challenges with them that are extraordinarily difficult to address. Regardless, assigning blame is a fruitless exercise. With the right strategies and effort, it is possible to get much higher graduation rates, and that, rather than finding fault with either students or schools, should be our focus.

SCOPE

This book is intended to inform policy and practice at any level, from individual high schools to national systems. The suggestions or proposals being made are all for things that could be done in most (if not all) schools, by ordinary educators working with a reasonable level of effort and skill. In other words, they are possible in schools as we find them today.

Although this book is directed largely toward North American school systems, it draws on experience and research from many different countries. Comparative studies and analyses can help us understand our own settings and think about alternatives that could work.

Forms of secondary education differ in important ways from one country to another, and each country or province has its own ecology of schooling that includes not only a range of education policies but also the way those policies interact with other social factors such as public attitudes, the structure of postsecondary education, or the labor market. Single policies should not be imported from other places without understanding the context in which they appear to succeed; to do otherwise is to risk the same results as are achieved by importing a foreign species into an environment. Almost always, the result is unexpected and bad. To argue that Country X is successful and has external exams or autonomous schools so we should do the same is rarely a good or successful strategy.

A similar approach applies to the use of research evidence. In general, education makes inadequate use of empirical research; we tend to be far too ready to try something new and faddish instead of relying on substantive bodies of evidence to guide policy and practice. While there are many areas where we do not have enough good evidence, there are many other areas, noted throughout the book, where there is good evidence that is not used. The ideas in this book are largely tested through experience, but they are also consistent with the best available research.

Many examples are included of these actions in real systems. At the same time, because the focus is on changes that could be made in any school or system, I do not include examples that cannot be replicated across large numbers of schools. Thus, schools that have extraordinary leadership, have managed to recruit the best teachers from a whole area, or have substantial amounts of additional funding are not discussed here because they do not provide examples that could be used by just about any school, anywhere. Similarly, copying programs or policies from other schools is not enough unless they are part of a coherent and comprehensive strategy.

In order to keep the book readable, I have avoided extensive referencing. However, the book does have many references, as well as links to many useful websites.

HOW HIGH CAN WE AIM?

The expansion of education is one of the remarkable stories of the last century. A hundred years ago, universal public education was relatively new. Most students received between four and six years of very basic education under conditions that would now widely be seen as unacceptable, such as very large classes and physical punishment. Fifty years ago, completion of high school was still a credential for a minority. Today, graduation from high school is now a basic educational qualification in much of the world, in the same way that elementary schooling was 50 years ago.

The rhetoric about education policy is often framed in economic terms, about what is required for work in the modern economy and therefore, for the country's economic welfare. These outcomes are important. A person who cannot participate effectively in the skilled economy will have a hard time earning a decent income and supporting a family. But higher levels of education are about much more than economic success, important as that is. Today's—and tomorrow's—democracies need, more than ever, citizens with a broad understanding of history, science, economics, politics, ethics, and psychology. As Einstein said, "You cannot solve a problem with the same sort of thinking that created the problem in the first place." This means that we need more people who are more educated than ever before.

The two greatest challenges facing our planet are our ability to preserve the physical environment and our ability to live together peacefully with others who are different. These challenges are not primarily economic. They call for people with deep understanding, good values, and the ability to live with change and uncertainty. Even at a more modest level, living in the world today requires an understanding of what to eat, how to raise children, how to look after one's health, and what choices the larger society should make. Today, we need almost everyone to reach levels of knowledge and understanding that, within our lifetimes, were once reserved for a few. The requirements for good education today more than ever require critical thinking, analytic skills, interpersonal skills, and humility. These are deep-seated educational values going back thousands of years. There has never been more alignment between traditional education values and the economic and social rationales for higher levels of education.

All of this is why levels of high school completion that would have been seen as impossible to reach a few decades ago are now seen as insufficient. Expectations have increased very, very quickly.

Nor is this simply a matter of having a high school graduation diploma, since considerable evidence shows that there are economic and social benefits to individuals and societies for actual skill levels, even after taking formal credentials into account. Graduates with higher levels of literacy will tend to get better jobs, earn more, and live longer than graduates with fewer skills (Hanushek & Wossman, 2007). One fundamental theme in improving high school outcomes is, therefore, that graduation must be the result of real skill development. We do students no favor by giving them credentials that do not indicate substantive learning.

In short, we are asking our schools to *bring more students than ever before to higher levels of attainment than ever before, on a broader range of skills than ever before, and with less inequity than ever before.*

That is a tall order but also an exciting one. If framed and implemented appropriately, it can appeal deeply to the public and to educators. Citizens and taxpayers already believe that high school graduation is essential for all young people, and they want that graduation to be meaningful in terms of skills and knowledge. An ambitious goal can also revitalize educators. People go into teaching to make the world a better place and to help students achieve important goals. Sometimes these early motivations get lost along the way because the daily routine hides the larger purpose, or because other life events distract people from their careers. Reestablishing those earlier altruistic views can be helpful and powerful. Appealing to the ideals of educators, as long as the appeals are not empty or cynical, is part of an effective education improvement strategy; much more effective than attacking people for being lazy or threatening to fire them.

Is the goal reasonable, though? How much can we expect from students? It is easy to talk about "all students graduating" or "all students reaching proficiency," but in reality, there is much disagreement among educators and the general population about these goals. Many people, including many teachers, remain convinced that human ability is fixed, and that the only way we can have more graduates is by lowering standards. These beliefs are not just slogans; they are deeply embedded in many educational practices such as grading on a curve, norm-referenced tests (which assume that a certain portion of students should or will do poorly), limited access to high-status programs, strict controls on the movement of students in schools, and so on. They are also linked, in ways discussed a little later, to the structure of rewards in our society, which only has a limited number of places for highly successful people. Secondary schools in particular face a double standard of public judgment. If failure rates are too high, schools are accused of doing a poor job, but if success rates get too high, schools may be accused of lowering standards. This catch-22 is a serious challenge for improving secondary education.

Fortunately, whatever public or professional beliefs may be, the question of young people's potential is an issue on which we have quite a bit of evidence, and the evidence indicates strongly that given motivation and the right supports, most people are capable of much higher levels of achievement in virtually every sphere than they or others think.

Consider how educational attainment has increased over time. Many people alive today can remember a time when graduation from high school was the exception, not the rule, and only a small minority of students went on to postsecondary education. In the United States in 1900, 6% of 17-year-olds finished high school; by 1970, about half began some type of postsecondary education (Abbott, 1988), and today the goal is graduation for all. The same is now true around the world. In comparing education systems in its member countries, the OECD (2009) reports the proportion of students in an age cohort who can be expected to complete secondary education or its equivalent by their early 20s. The OECD average is 80%, with several countries above 95%. These numbers would have been inconceivable to our grandparents. They cannot be compared too literally, because "graduation" means somewhat different things in different places. Still, they show that high school graduation is now common in all these countries and that there are countries where virtually all students attain a qualification that has value for further education, work, or both.

Consider, also, how quickly these numbers can change. Korea and Singapore are countries that, fifty years ago, had quite low levels of education. In Korea, only about 40% of those now ages 55 to 64 completed their secondary education in the late 1960s and early 1970s. Forty years later, well over 90% of Korean young people are completing secondary school. In one generation, the country transformed itself educationally. Singapore started with even lower rates and now graduates virtually all of its high school students. The same sort of increase happened in North America from the 1920s through the 1960s but has not been sustained since then.

It is not just overall attainment that has risen either. The educational attainment of females, of various minority groups, or of people with various disabilities has risen even more dramatically as each new group demonstrated its capacity to benefit from public education, often after centuries in which it was assumed that they could not do so or that extending their education would threaten the very basis of society. In the early days of public education, leaders assumed, quite wrongly, that working-class or immigrant children could not succeed. The arguments made a century ago against the education of women now seem preposterous, but they were widely accepted at the time because many men either believed that women would not benefit from education or, perhaps, feared that they would benefit too much! Similar arguments have been made more recently about minorities or people with disabilities but have been eventually refuted by the facts of performance of these groups when given the right opportunities. Yet the beliefs have pernicious effects because they lead to the denial of real opportunity.

Yet another reason for optimism has to do with the variance in graduation rates among schools and in the United States, among states. Virtually all studies show that schools with similar demographics can have very different success rates. A 2010 study in New York found that student success varied enormously across schools, even with similar students. In schools that enrolled those with the lowest prior achievement, the on-time graduation rate ranged from 34% to 90%; the rate of students in these schools earning Regents Diplomas, which signify adequate preparation for college or the workplace, ranged from zero to 83% (Campaign for Fiscal Equity, 2010).

The same is true of states. According to Balfanz, Bridgeland, Moore, and Fox (2010), state high school graduation rates in 2008 ranged from nearly 90% (e.g., Wisconsin, Vermont) to below 60% (e.g., Louisiana, Mississippi, Nevada). A study by the Education Testing Service a few years earlier (Barton, 2005) concluded that 60% of this variation was explained statistically by socioeconomic (SES) characteristics of the students, suggesting that a considerable amount of this gap could potentially be overcome by different approaches in schools. Moreover, we have increasing evidence that whole systems can make progress in relatively short periods of time. New York and Tennessee increased their graduation rates by more than 10% from 2002 to 2008 (Balfanz et al., 2010). The province of Ontario increased its graduation rate from 68% to 81% between 2005 and 2010. In each case, this meant many thousands more students graduating each year; students who, presumably, would have been thought incapable of that success only a few years earlier.

Even more compelling is the evidence from studies of individuals. More is said on this point a little later, but it is safe to say that virtually every study of this matter shows that a very significant number of students with poor achievement at one point in their career will eventually reach quite satisfactory levels of attainment (e.g., Barton, 2005). Although teachers believe that they can predict which students will succeed later in life and which will not, the evidence is that such predictions are often inaccurate. This ability to turn things around is the educational equivalent of resilience generally, which tells us that people can have good life outcomes even if they have some very serious early hardships, provided that they have some of the right supports— the most notable of which is caring adults in their lives. In international comparisons (OECD, 2010b), the most successful countries are those that support and encourage this resilience, allowing more students to outperform the predictions based on their demographics.

The conclusion we can draw from these various findings is that we simply do not know the limits of student potential, either for individuals or for populations. All we know for sure is that we have not reached them yet. We should be highly optimistic that with the right efforts, our young people can get better results.

NOT ALL SOLUTIONS ARE GOOD ONES

Proposals for improving high schools abound and have for decades. One could fill a large room with reports on the problem of dropouts, proposals as to what to do about it, and evaluations of pilot projects intended to improve high school outcomes. Anyone writing a book such as this, which purports to give advice on improving high school outcomes, should be humbled by the record of earlier advice—both the quantity given and the poor results from most of it. Indeed, many of the ideas in this book concerning engaging students, independent learning, and community connections were in quite wide use in the late 1960s and early 1970s, only to fade away in subsequent decades.

It is easy to list dozens of remedies that have been confidently prescribed as the way to generate better results. For example, the creation of vocational schools and vocational programs was a response to student diversity and disaffection from traditional academic programs but often led to dead-end programs. Minimum competency tests were widely prescribed and implemented in the 1980s, without much result. Lately, the proposal has been the opposite—that all students should pursue a common curriculum, typically focused mainly on traditional academics. Or as another example, at one time, larger schools were recommended as a way to offer a wider range of courses of interest to more students. Smaller schools were recommended to offset the alienation of large schools.

One of the great temptations in education policy is to find a single solution that will fix everything. As H. L. Mencken said, "There is always a well-known solution to every human problem—neat, plausible, and wrong" (www.quotationspage.com/quote/26687.html). However, that does not prevent simple fixes from being proposed repeatedly—largely because they appeal to both policy-makers and voters. In politics, the words "it's very complicated" are not calculated to win over voters, especially when compared to "I have the answer." Nor should we blame politicians for this. They are motivated by what citizens will accept and pay attention to; if we get simplistic policies, it is because we vote for them!

It is tempting—oh so tempting!—to believe that we can improve school outcomes by changing some external element. If we only we had higher standards for all students. If only we had more or better tests. If we only had more choice or competition or charter schools. If only we had merit pay for teachers. If we only could get rid of teacher unions. If only we could hire whoever we wanted to teach. If only we could close all the worst schools. And so on.

A full discussion of the evidence involved would require another book, but the reality is that not one of those frequent proposals is supported by good evidence—by which I mean independent evidence from multiple sources that this strategy consistently produces improvement across a school system, including reducing achievement gaps. Most successful school systems around the world use few, if any, of those strategies. As was clearly shown at a "summit" on teaching and teachers hosted in March, 2011 by the U.S. Department of Education (U.S. Department of Education, 2011), the countries with the best international performance of students are not achieving success based on testing, competition among schools, bashing teachers, or eliminating unions (Fullan, 2011). They understand that one cannot change institutional performance in schools just through changing structures or incentives, and they all have positive and comprehensive strategies in place (Asia Society, 2011).

WHY NOT LEAVE SCHOOLS ALONE TO FIGURE IT OUT?

If most of the top-down reforms proposed so far have not worked well, a bottom-up strategy also has shortcomings. Several jurisdictions have attempted strategies that relied on the efforts of individual schools to develop their own strategies custom-made to their own context and challenges. The idea behind these approaches is that educators themselves are best able to define what is needed and bring it about, so the solution is to give schools more autonomy coupled with more accountability.

Unfortunately, the evidence does not support this approach either. A recent example comes from the Canadian province of Quebec, which has very high results on the Programme for International Student Assessment (PISA) tests but also has an alarmingly low high school graduation rate—even though high school there ends after Grade 11, not 12. In 2002, the provincial government launched a major initiative to improve graduation rates, relying heavily on initiatives taken by individual schools. A recently released evaluation (Janosz, 2010) shows that the initiatives had relatively little impact on student achievement, primarily because there was not enough external support for schools so that instructional practice hardly changed at all.

The same conclusion has been reached in various other studies of school-driven improvement efforts in various countries. For example, California provided extra funding to high-need schools from 2001 to 2004, but an evaluation (Harr, Parrish, Socias, & Gubbins, 2007) showed that the program had little effect on student outcomes and, as in Quebec, schools had very limited ability to design and implement high-quality changes. Moreover, countries with highly decentralized systems, such as the United Kingdom or New Zealand, do not seem to have particularly better outcomes or levels of improvement occurring after that decentralization. In England, real improvement came when the system began to focus on improvement in the late 1990s, not in the 1980s when it moved to decentralization and school choice.

On reflection, the idea that every school will know what to do to improve outcomes seems rather unrealistic. It presumes that this knowledge has been there all along and only outside constraints have prevented these schools from taking the actions they know to be right. That is a hard proposition to swallow. It is much more likely that schools either do not know what changes to make or lack the capacity to make them.

Moreover, schools in most places are not autonomous agencies. They are embedded in districts or other systems that shape and constrain what they do. Many studies show how much districts influence what happens in individual schools. As one example, Hargreaves and Fink (2006) describe how a district's decision to replace a principal or to change a key policy may dramatically affect what happens in its schools. At a more mundane but no less important level, Johnson (2004) shows how district hiring procedures can make it very difficult for schools to staff effectively.

In other cases, districts may move principals around in ways that do not support lasting improvement. Insofar as schools are not independent actors, improvement must be embedded in school systems as well—what Michael Fullan (2007) calls the "tri-level solution."

Another reason to think more systemically is the need for all schools, not just some, to focus on improvement. There has been much discussion lately in the United States about "failure factories," a relatively small number of schools that are held to turn out a large portion of dropouts. It is true that some schools have much bigger problems than others and require more extensive and intensive action to reach an adequate level of outcomes for students. However, a central theme of this book is that system improvement is just that—it involves every school getting better. The fact is that very large numbers of unsuccessful students are in schools that are achieving decent overall results, and if all the focus is on low-performing schools, those students will be missed. A little elementary math makes this clear.

Let's suppose the worst 10% of schools, with 20% of all students (since they are typically large, urban schools) are the scene of vastly disproportionate levels of failure—where as few as 40% of students are graduating appropriately instead of 70%. Simple calculation shows that these schools are still producing only 40% of the failures; 60% are in other schools. So while very poor performing schools do need attention, the problem of poor high school graduation rates cannot be solved by focusing just on the bottom-performing schools. We do students a disservice if we assume that the problem is located only in a few schools, and we run the risk that other schools will see the problem as belonging to someone else. All schools have students who are missing out, and all schools need to work on improving.

WHY SCHOOL IS NOT LIKE WORK AND WHY STUDENTS SHOULD NOT BE TREATED LIKE WORKERS

Many proposals for improving secondary schools suggest that the treatment of schools should emulate workplaces. Workers cannot come to work late or fail to hand in assignments without serious consequences, so, it is argued, the same should apply to students in schools in order to prepare them for the realities of work and life.

There are serious flaws in this argument. The comparison between students and workers is a poor one. Most fundamentally, students do not agree to go to school in exchange for a salary, which is the situation of virtually all workers. In a workplace, employees agree to abide by the rules in exchange for payment, and the workplace is not there in the first instance for the welfare of workers. However, students are not paid to go to school, and the whole purpose of the institution is precisely to advance their interests. So the analogy fails in an important way.

Perhaps more important, the goal of school is to improve students' skills, attitudes, and knowledge. This is not the goal of a workplace, although it may be something workplaces pay attention to in order to be successful in other ways. It is possible to imagine a workplace in which employees get nothing of value other than their wages; indeed, many if not most workplaces in history have been of that nature. It is nonsensical to imagine a school like that for students, since that would be antithetical to the whole idea of school. In a school, everything should be organized around what is likely to produce the most lasting learning for students, in line with the objectives and goals of the education system. In that sense, students are much more like the customers in a business than they are like the staff, although the analogy to customers is also an unhelpful one for many reasons.

Consider someone learning a skill, such as a pilot, surgeon, or plumber. Nobody expects that learner to get things right the first time. In fact, education in these areas consists of continual practice under close supervision, until the skill is learned. Novice pilots can crash their simulator airplanes over and over until they can land the plane safely every time. Moreover, people are not punished because they started poorly and then improved; nobody suggests rating a surgeon as mediocre because she was not very good at the start of her training, whereas by the end, she is highly competent. The only thing that matters is the final level of skill or knowledge, similar to someone learning a language. We expect people to start with minimal skill and then to improve over time; it makes no sense to lower our assessment of them because they did not know much when they started out.

In many other areas as well, schools do not embody the operating principles of most workplaces. Few workplaces control employee behavior the way schools monitor and control students, and those that do tend to have high levels of staff turnover, since talented people want autonomy in their work. In workplaces, people are given real tasks to do, not assignments that are intended only for a teacher. In most workplaces today, people work together, so using and building on the ideas and skills of others is considered valuable, not cheating. One could go on, but the point should be clear: students should not be thought of as workers in an enterprise, and schools are not workplaces in that sense either; they should, in all ways, be governed by the logic flowing from their educational purposes. Because schools have a different purpose, solutions to school issues must be based on educational thinking, not models borrowed from other sectors.

CAN HIGH SCHOOLS BE TRANSFORMED?

Another current proposal for schools could be described as *transformation*. This is the idea that high schools are obsolete institutions that embody a vanished industrial world, and that they need to be changed fundamentally. Although such proposals are often short on details, they typically suggest some combination of more independent learning, more learning in the broader community, and more use of technology, such as virtual schools (e.g., Wagner, 2008). Bill Gates's observation in February 2005 to U.S. governors about the obsolescence of high schools is often invoked to make this point (Summit, 2005).

I have some sympathy with this argument. In many ways, high schools are not well-suited to the contemporary world. However, the focus in this book is on improving the schools we have rather than on trying to create entirely new forms of secondary education. I take this position for an intensely practical reason: there is no sign that there will be any large-scale transformation of secondary schooling. The call for a transformed high school is not new; it has been made for at least 40 years now, yet nowhere in the world is secondary education being changed in dramatic ways for large numbers of students. Where there has been improvement, it has occurred through incremental change, not transformation.

Frequent breakthroughs are trumpeted, with the growing enrollment in virtual schools and the use of PDAs being the latest in a long line. It may be that at some point, there will be a real shift in how high school education is designed, and that could be a very good thing. In the meantime, the tens of thousands of people working in secondary schools, and the millions of students attending them, need our best efforts to improve the existing institutions.

WHY STUDENTS DON'T GRADUATE

A sound approach to improvement should start with a clear understanding of the problem. To improve graduate rates, we must examine why students do not graduate now. Thousands of studies have addressed the question of why students fail to complete secondary school. This large body of research has supported some conventional wisdom on dropouts but has also called into question other commonly held views about why students leave and what it would take for them to stay and succeed.

Many factors may affect students' failure to complete secondary school. These factors may relate to students themselves and their families, to the school, or to the relationship between the two. What the studies show is that failure to graduate is usually the result of a whole set of influences that affect children from early in their lives through their entire school careers. As many researchers describe it, failing to graduate, or "dropping out," is a process, not an event.

Various aspects of students' home environment, such as their parents' education and occupation, are quite strong predictors of how well students do in school. Although we tend to measure these factors independently, in practice, multiple forces influence each other. For example, it is not so much lower income in itself that matters but the things that result from or are related to lower income, such as more instability in living conditions, increased stress on parents, fewer resources in the home, perhaps poorer nutrition or health care, and so on. Lower income may itself be the result of other factors as well, such as mental or physical health issues or systemic discrimination in the labor market.

While student background is a powerful influence on educational and other life outcomes, the strengths and limitations that children bring to school may be helped or hindered by features of the school itself. In the United States, there is much evidence that schools with the most challenged students may receive less funding and have less qualified or experienced teachers, making it harder to support students, even though their students are most in need of such support (Darling-Hammond, 2010; Education Trust, 2008; see also the Education Trust website: www.edtrust .org/dc/resources/publications/funding-fairness).

Once students begin their school careers, various warning signs emerge that suggest problems ahead. Students who struggle with basic skills in the primary grades, who are held back in elementary school, who are placed in special education, whose attendance is poor, who change schools frequently, or whose families are unable to provide the necessary stability, support, and advocacy all face much greater challenges and a lower probability of success.

Schools and teachers are well aware of these influences. After all, they see them every day. Nothing is more frustrating to a teacher than a student who doesn't show up or seems to make no effort to learn. The propensity of educators to place responsibility for lack of success on students or their families is entirely understandable and consistent with quite a bit of research. That is why so many teachers believe that they can predict with great accuracy what a student's future will be.

The problem is that this tendency is both wrong and dangerous. It is wrong because probabilities do not determine individual outcomes, and it is dangerous because knowing about students' background challenges and previous school record can, and often does, produce behavior that reinforces negative attitudes and behavior, thus creating more of the problem instead of trying to remedy it.

This point is so important that it requires some elaboration. How can it be wrong to use research that shows very high correlations between factors such as students' attendance or their elementary school achievement and their high school graduation? A closer look at the evidence shows that although many factors are strongly related to the likelihood of dropping out, no single factor is strong enough to be used for prediction within a school. This point seems counterintuitive, so it needs a little explication. The problem lies in the concept of probabilities. High correlations are important and powerful, but they are far from perfect.

In social sciences, a relationship of .7 between, say, students' socioeconomic background and completion of high school would be considered very strong. But if used to try to predict individual outcomes in a system that had, say, a 60% graduation rate (as in Table 1.1 below), a factor with a .7 correlation would correctly predict fewer than 60% of student outcomes. In other words, predictions based on that relationship would be wrong two-thirds as often as they were correct, which is hardly adequate.

This is why the National Dropout Prevention Center (Hammond, Linton, Smink, & Drew, 2007) concluded, as have many other studies, that no single factor can or should be used to predict failure to graduate from high school.

But even using multiple predictors together is not all that helpful when it comes to looking at a particular school and students. Gleason and Dynarski (2002) found that even a regression analysis using 40 variables to predict student outcomes was wrong more than it was right when used to predict outcomes for individual students!

It is also the case that students themselves, when asked, have high aspirations for their futures. At age 14, 15, or even 16, the vast majority of students envisage good futures for themselves, often including postsecondary education (National Research Council, 2003). Then something happens to them to change their path so that many of them do not reach those desired futures.

It is widely assumed that those who fail to graduate do so primarily because of academic difficulties (they are failing too many courses), personal challenges (such as highly disruptive home lives), or some combination of the two. Of course, these are important reasons that do affect large numbers of students, but by no means all. A considerable number of students who fail

Table 1.1   Accuracy of Predictions About Students Based on a Correlation of .7

Outcome Predicted/ Actual	Actually Graduated—70%	Did Not Graduate—30%
Predicted graduate—70%	$.7 \times .7 = 49\%$—Correct	$.7 \times .3 = 21\%$— Incorrect
Predicted not to graduate—30%	$.3 \times .7 = 21\%$— Incorrect	$.3 \times .3 = 9\%$—Correct

to graduate have not received any failing grades; if they did not earn the necessary credits, it was because they lost interest and stopped attending or handing in work. When they did complete work, it was quite satisfactory. Indeed, a longitudinal Alberta study (Nadirova & Burger, 2009) showed that some substantial portions of students who had no risk factors, including 10% of students identified as gifted in third grade, failed to graduate from high school.

Here is another example: Canada conducted a longitudinal study (OECD and Statistics Canada, 2010) of students who took the OECD's PISA test in 2000 at age 15 (mostly in 10th grade). PISA divides students' literacy scores into five levels, with 5 being very high and 1 being very low (equivalent to an elementary school level). In 2006, these students were followed up at age 21. Of those who scored Level 5, more than 90% were in or had completed postsecondary education, as one might expect. However, of those students who were rated at Level 1 literacy in 2000, nearly 40% were in postsecondary education six years later, even though Level 1 reading would have been a very strong indicator that they lacked the skills for success in postsecondary education.

Earlier, we reviewed some of the evidence suggesting that schools with very similar populations often have very different outcomes in terms of student achievement and graduation rates; this also suggests that the demographic indicators that are often used to predict success are far from immutable. Every study of schools or students shows that there is high variance in success among schools with very similar demographics, as well as among students in those schools with similar demographics, including levels of prior achievement. Statisticians describe this finding by saying that the variance within any group is usually bigger than the variance between any two groups. So, for example, there is much more variance in achievement among boys or among girls than there is between boys and girls on average. Similarly, high SES schools on average will have better outcomes than low SES schools, but the gap among high SES schools or among low SES schools is usually bigger than the average gap between the two groups of schools.

All of this brings us to three conclusions. The first is that spending a lot of time on trying to predict who is "at risk" or more likely to drop out is not a very good use of resources. Of course, schools should be cognizant of the factors that are more strongly related to leaving school early, but analyses of risk factors is not a good route to more success. Second, the evidence shows that schools can have significant effects on student outcomes, no matter who their students are. This is a very positive conclusion, since if it were not the case, if students' background predestined them to particular outcomes, then it would not be clear why we would want to invest substantial resources in high schools. Third, efforts to increase graduation rates cannot just be focused on particular categories of students or on certain kinds of schools. Instead, it is essential to be thoughtful about each student who is struggling, taking into consideration the context of each school and community.

Having made that point, it is equally important to say that schools and school systems are not responsible for the inequalities in society generally and that it is entirely unfair to expect schools to remedy those inequalities entirely on their own. Educators are right to resent the implication that if they only worked harder, they could compensate for all the ills of society. That is why educators and their organizations should also be advocates for changes in the larger society that will make their work more successful by reducing inequities in work, wages, housing, health care, and other areas important to the welfare of young people and families (Rothstein, 2004). That advocacy is important, but the task of the schools still remains. The point of view in this book is that schools cannot do everything, but they can do some things, often more than they think. Everyone involved in education must do what they can in their own situation, while at the same time advocating for a better society overall.

THE ROLE OF PRE-HIGH SCHOOL AND WHY FOCUS ON HIGH SCHOOLS

Many proposals concerning improved high school graduation rates suggest beginning in junior high or even in elementary schools. After all, the argument goes, if students get a stronger beginning, they will likely do better later in their schooling as well.

Of course, good beginnings for students are important. I am an advocate for strong early childhood programs, especially support for parents and children from prenatal to age two or three.

These efforts have been shown to have very high returns (Karoly, Kilburn, & Cannon, 2005). Similarly, strong primary programs are important in getting students off to a good start.

The danger in placing too much emphasis on these earlier levels is that it has the potential to cause people in high schools to think there is little they can do if students arrive with serious problems or deficiencies. Yet we know that people can make progress in their lives at any age. High schools must take on the challenge of the students they have, not just wish they had different ones.

WHY HIGH SCHOOLS ARE HARD TO CHANGE

One of the striking features of the literature on school and system change is the consensus on how hard it is to create lasting change in secondary schools (Earl, Torrance, & Sutherland, 2006). Studies of system change in Chicago, San Diego, Boston, Philadelphia, and other large U.S. cities have drawn this conclusion. For example, in Chicago, the improvements in elementary schools in the 1990s were not mirrored at all in secondary schools (Bryk, Sebring, Allensworth, Luppescu, & Easton, 2010). So despite many accounts of individual teachers or principals who overcame difficulties to build success in their schools, most experts would say that we know much less about creating lasting and meaningful improvement in high schools than we do for elementary schools.

There are several reasons why it is harder to create improvement in high schools than in elementary schools. Unless we understand these barriers and think about how to address them, improvement strategies for high schools will be wrongly designed and will continue to founder. Moreover, these challenges have to be seen as an integrated set; dealing with just one of them will not succeed because the other barriers remain.

The first important difference is the size of the organization. Everywhere, high schools are bigger, often much bigger, than elementary schools. Whereas many elementary schools around the world have a few hundred students, high schools often have 1,000 students, and some are much larger than that. In Ontario, the average elementary school has about 325 students, while the typical high school has about 1,000. Change in a larger organization means having more people involved and on-site and also much more complicated communications challenges; keeping 60 or 80 teachers and 20 or 30 other staff fully informed and engaged is quite a different challenge than doing the same with 15 teachers and five support staff.

Partly as a result of size, the leadership role is different in high schools. School principals don't have the same direct connection with daily teaching and learning, not only because there are more teachers and students but also because the administrative and management requirements are greater. This means a different approach to leadership in secondary schools is needed, an issue discussed more in later chapters.

Secondary schools are also much more centered on subjects than are elementary schools. The organization of secondary schools by subjects has many implications for improvement. Teachers may have more allegiance to their subjects than to the school as an organization. The old aphorism is that elementary teachers love their students while secondary teachers love their subjects (and university professors love themselves, someone suggested!). Of course, many secondary teachers are deeply committed to their students, but subject areas are the basis on which timetables, budgets, teacher assignments, and other structural features are organized. Coupled with size, this means that many teachers may not have a good sense of developments across the school as a whole and may not even have a strong interest in the school as a whole.

Subject divisions matter not only organizationally but also in terms of attitudes and cultures. Some subject groups—often the core subjects such as English, math, or science—may feel themselves to be central to the enterprise while seeing others as less important or less "academic." One colleague of mine reported working in a high school where teachers in core academic subjects referred to teachers in some other areas, such as vocational education, as "NRTs," meaning "not real teachers." If some groups feel marginalized in the school, they may resist various schoolwide improvement strategies.

Different departments in high schools may also have quite different orientations toward students and teaching. This subject-linked view may also have to do with appropriate teaching strategies and ways of working with students (for example, willingness to use principles of formative assessment), views on the use of examinations, or even views as to which students belong in their courses and classes. It can be difficult to generate a whole-school approach to supporting students if, for example, some teachers feel that their subject has always had and should have a 50% failure rate as a sign of its rigor. Often these views are deeply held by teachers and cannot be washed away by a couple of all-staff planning sessions.

Another important structural element of high schools is the greater diversity in high school students' achievement levels and orientations to schooling compared to elementary school students. The truism is that in a school, the variation in students' achievement is roughly equal to the grade level. That means that in first grade there may already be about a year's difference in achievement among students in a class, while by 10th grade the gap is much, much wider. The greater the variance in students' skills, the harder it is to organize teaching effectively and the more pressure there is to create different classes or programs for students who are behind academically. Since their inception, high schools have struggled with what to do with students who are not particularly interested in standard academic work or who are far behind others in their skills. The usual response has been some version of *tracking* or *streaming,* in which different courses or programs are created with the intent of suiting the different needs, interests, and aptitudes of some students.

The problem with tracking—discussed more fully in Chapter 4—is that its effects on outcomes have been pernicious, a finding now well-established by research. The doctrine of "separate but equal" does not work any better in high school program structures than it did in race relations. In practice, in the minds of teachers, students, and parents, high school program streams are differentiated by value related to difficulty, not by their match to student needs or interests.

Tracks and streams continue to exist, though, and have important implications for the organization of the school, for teaching, and for student relations. Which teachers are assigned to which courses becomes a vital issue in determining whether the highest-need students get the best teaching. Schools have to position themselves to their public in terms of the programs they offer and, to some extent, the kinds of students they want to attract. Counselors and parents have the difficult challenge of assigning students to appropriate courses without falling into the trap of low expectations, especially for minority groups. All the evidence shows that our record in resolving any of these challenges is not very good and that tracking decisions are also affected by extraneous factors, such as ethnicity or gender (Gamoran, 2009; Oakes, 2005).

The issue of tracking and streaming is made more difficult by the role of high schools in shaping students' futures through access to postsecondary education and employment. If students are asked why they go to high school, few will respond by noting their love of learning. Their purposes are mainly instrumental, reinforced by the way adults talk to them about schooling: to graduate, to qualify for postsecondary education, to be able to get the kind of job they want, or to earn the income they want.

Whatever our rhetoric about schools as places of learning, everyone understands that high schools are also about shaping who gets what later in life. This access is limited by the nature of the society and economy; in no society are there enough places for everyone to have his or her preferred future. The best opportunities are rationed. Harvard only takes so many students; there are only so many jobs for pilots or doctors. High school grades are a key determinant in entry to those futures, which means that high schools, whether they wish to be or not, are gatekeepers for students' access to opportunities.

One consequence of the limitations of access is that high schools inevitably have a competitive element to them. It is easy to imagine (though not at all easy to achieve) a system in which virtually every child can read competently at age 12. It is not easy even to imagine high schools in which all students reach high levels of achievement on demanding curricula. Who would get into Ivy League colleges, and who would go to local junior colleges or technical schools? Even if one accepts that there is an increasing need for high skill levels in modern economies, every economy still generates a large number of low-wage service jobs. If all students reached high levels of skill, who would want, or be willing, to earn minimum wage working as security guards or fast-food servers? Many countries have addressed this problem by importing workers to take on low-wage, low-skill work, but this produces its own problems in the form of illegal immigrants or people who feel no real allegiance to a country that does not allow them to share fully in its wealth and success. On the other hand, countries that produce much higher numbers of graduates than their economies can absorb run the risk of considerable disaffection when educated young people cannot find work commensurate with their skills. Do we want people with PhDs driving taxis?

Where rewards are limited, competition is a central element. Only some can win, which means others must lose. The competitive nature of high school education changes the way that students and teachers think about what they are doing and how they work with each other. Sometimes the result is more effort, but sometimes it is beggar-thy-neighbor or lower expectations. High schools also have important influences on students' sense of their own competence, which may affect their effort and their aspirations for their future. Students who struggle in school are more likely to lower their own future goals as a result. At age 12 or 14, most students still have high expectations for their own futures; by age 16, these have been considerably moderated for some students.

Of course, high schools also exhibit some of the barriers that have been challenges for improvement in elementary schools. One of these is the attribution of success and failure—the belief among many educators that students' performance is limited by their background, despite the evidence discussed earlier that we generally underestimate people's potential, and often by a considerable amount. Especially in communities with high levels of poverty or large minority or immigrant populations, the risk that the schools will reduce their expectations for their students remains high (e.g., Muijs, Harris, Chapman, Stoll, & Russ, 2004).

A second challenge at all levels of education is the deeply rooted romantic faith in individualism—the notion that every school or teacher has, and should have, a unique way of doing things, to be discovered from experience and sometimes through "reflection." The belief in "teacher autonomy" has no parallel in other professions. Indeed, the essence of a profession is that members share common beliefs and practices. Membership implies a commitment to doing the work in ways that the profession as a whole has come to regard, through a combination of experience and research, as being the correct ways to proceed. Of course, there is always a large element of professional judgment in how these rules or procedures are applied in particular situations. That is the skill that a professional possesses. But other professions reject the idea that an individual practitioner can choose to disregard the larger knowledge base on account of an individual predisposition. No other profession would suggest that professional development ought to belong entirely to individuals and that it is pernicious for the larger system to require particular practices where these are well-grounded in evidence. Yet many educators continue to argue against practices or approaches being required of all teachers, no matter how strong the evidence behind them. That position not only weakens teaching from the standpoint of effectiveness, but it also makes schools open to any crackpot idea that comes along, since there is no agreed-on practice based on shared and validated professional knowledge.

All of this discussion should be moderated by the understanding that students are the active creators of their own lives, not just passive raw materials to be worked on by adults, whether in schools or elsewhere. That kind of discussion has the effect of reducing students to passive subjects of their situation, which is both incorrect and mischievous. To be sure, students create their own lives in a particular context that shapes and constrains, sometimes severely, what they see as possible and what is really possible for them. Still, as discussed earlier, there is a great deal of evidence that people's hopes can be reignited with very powerful and positive results at almost any age. All of this means that schools need to pay very careful attention to who their students are, what students think and what they see as the possibilities in their lives, and how schools can help all students, especially those who are struggling, to lift their sights—to want, pursue, and achieve more for themselves.

CONCLUSION

This chapter set out to describe the challenge of improving high school graduation rates. It reviewed the remarkable and successful expansion of public education over the last century, coupled with ever-rising expectations for high schools and growing evidence that most students are capable of more than most of us think. It discussed the limitations of many current proposals for reforming high schools and, to set the stage for the ideas to follow, reviewed the reasons that students do not graduate and the challenges in the nature of high schools that makes them so hard to improve in a systemic way. All of this sets the groundwork for the main purpose of this book, which is to set out powerful, yet feasible, strategies that will help many more students graduate and increase their opportunities to play a full and successful role in life.

Take-Aways

- We do not yet know the limits of our students' capacity to learn and grow, but we have much evidence that with the right motivation and support, most people are capable of more, often much more, than they or others thought. There is every reason to believe that we can have more success at higher levels for more students than we have today.

- Many of the ideas put forth to improve schools lack any sound base of evidence; in some cases, there is good evidence that these ideas make things worse rather than better.

- All schools, not just some, must be involved in improvement; however, neither a strict top-down nor a laissez-faire, bottom-up strategy can be successful.

- Whatever one thinks of the basic structure of high schools today, there is much evidence that results can be improved.

- Although background does predict students' outcomes, background is not destiny; we know that we can change students' futures because we already do so for many students.

- Structural features of high schools, such as their division into subjects and their strong connection to postsecondary education, make them difficult to change.

CHAPTER TWO

The Framework

The previous chapter set out the problems and challenges associated with helping more students graduate and pointed out that some of the most common proposals are not going to be enough in themselves. Changing a large and complex institution such as secondary schooling requires a multifaceted strategy. A look at systems that have made significant improvement shows that it is always the result of a comprehensive approach focused primarily on changing the real experiences of students.

The proposals in this book have grown out of research and experience. The research comes both from systems that have been more successful, particularly internationally, and from evidence on successful or rapidly improving systems. Additionally, I was intensively involved from 2004 through 2009 in designing and implementing the changes in Ontario, Canada, that led to a rapid and large increase in graduates (see text box).

The Ontario Student Success Strategy

Beginning in 2005, the Ontario government introduced a multi-element strategy to increase high school graduation rates.

The strategy is described in more detail in Levin, 2008. However, the main elements included the following:

- Creating dedicated infrastructures in the ministry and school boards, staffed by outstanding educators, to lead and guide the overall initiative

---

- Engaging school and district leaders to set ambitious but achievable targets and plans for increased student success

- Developing a "student success leadership team" in every school district and every school

- Providing extensive, carefully targeted professional development for educators to support the strategies

- Targeting attention to key underperforming groups, including some minority students, ESL students, students in special education, and Aboriginal students

- Supporting effective use of data to track students and intervene early when problems begin to occur

- Supporting a "student success teacher" in every high school as a champion for success for all students

- Building stronger transition models between elementary and secondary schools so students get off to a good start in high school

- Increasing the focus on (and resources for) literacy and numeracy in all areas of the high school curriculum

- Expanding program options through more cooperative education, credits for genuine external learning, and dual credit programs with colleges and universities

- Creating a "high-skills major" that allows school boards to work with employers and community groups to create packages of courses leading to real employment and further learning

- Introducing legislation to embody the changes in the overall strategy and also requiring students to be in a learning situation (school, college, apprenticeship, work with training, and so forth) until high school graduation or age 18

- Revising curricula in some key areas, such as mathematics and career education

- Creating a "student success commission" with representatives from the teacher federations, principals, and superintendents to support effective implementation of the strategy in schools and to prevent disputes at the local level

- Supporting research to find, understand, and share effective practices

- Supporting ancillary practices, such as an expansion of tutoring and fuller engagement of parents and communities

From 2004 to 2010, Ontario increased its five-year high school graduation rate from 68% to 81% meaning that by 2010, an additional 18,000 students each year were graduating in a timely manner from Ontario high schools compared to 2004. Not only that, but Ontario students are very high performers on international assessments, such as the Programme for International Student Assessment (PISA) and Trends in International Mathematics and Science Study (TIMSS), and have improved their performance in comparison with other students in Canada.

Though the specifics vary from one place to another, every system that has made significant gains in graduation rates has done so through a systematic, sustained effort that encompasses multiple facets of schooling with a particular focus on changing students' patterns of learning and achievement. No successful system has relied on a single approach such as accountability, school size, or curriculum, though these have often been parts of a more comprehensive approach. Every successful system has placed considerable emphasis on helping educators become more successful in their work, to the benefit of students, emphasizing what happens in schools more than the surrounding policy environment. The Ontario strategy, for example, included legislation to require students who had not graduated to be involved in learning until age 18. However, the legislation was important primarily as a symbol of intention. It was never thought of as a primary means of keeping students in school; that would be accomplished by changes in programs, teaching, and relationships.

One of the most sophisticated and interesting presentations of the interrelated nature of school change is the analysis of Chicago schools by Bryk, Sebring, Allensworth, Luppescu, and Easton (2010). They concluded that the primary focus must be on the experience of students and that this requires a multi-element strategy. The same point, even though the list of particulars varies, is made by many other experts and appears in virtually every important study of improvement. Changes in structures and incentives are often part of a strategy, but they are not enough by themselves. A multifaceted strategy, such as described in this book, is always needed to change a large and complex institution such as secondary schooling.

The argument in this book is that improving high school outcomes requires action on four fronts. These four strategies come out of an understanding of why students do not graduate, as discussed in the previous chapter. I first frame each of the main strategies in a single sentence, then I expand the discussion in the following chapters. The four core strategies are as follows:

1. Know the status and progress of every student, know the reasons for any problems, and intervene as soon as there are signs of difficulties.

2. Provide a program that enables all students to achieve a good outcome.

3. Improving daily teaching and learning is essential to achieving better high school outcomes; to do this requires a thoughtful and specific strategy.

4. Connect schools deeply to their local and broader community.

The organization of strategies under these four headings is only one way to think about the possibilities, of course. Other formulations have been made. For example, a recent report from a team led by Robert Balfanz (Balfanz, Bridgeland, Moore, & Fox, 2010), a leading U.S. expert on the dropout issue, proposed six main areas: data systems, adult advocates, academic support and enrichment, programs to improve academic performance, a personalized learning environment, and rigorous and relevant instruction to engage students.

Four focuses are proposed in this book because they provide a "recipe" that is clear and easy to remember for most educators. One of the essentials in any strategy for change is clear communication, and one of the essentials for clear communication is to keep the number of points few so that most people can keep them in mind.

It is essential to address all four areas if the goal of higher graduation rates is to be achieved. All are necessary to success. However, the order of discussion reflects both feasibility and importance. There is never enough time and resources to do everything; one has to choose those possibilities that combine the greatest impact with the least effort. Getting the right balance between these two criteria is one of the big challenges in organizational change. Feasibility is as important as impact; there is no point in tackling the "most important" strategy if it is too difficult to achieve; far better to take something that may have less effect but has much more possibility of success. That is why I start with connecting with every student, because this is likely to yield the biggest payoff for the least amount of effort.

That being said, all four areas of effort are interrelated and interdependent. For example, knowing and caring for students will not be enough if teaching and learning practices continue to result in disengaged learners. A report on high schools in Chicago (Allensworth & Easton, 2007) put it this way: "Students attend class more often when they have strong relationships with their teachers and when they see school and their coursework as relevant and important for their future" (p. 39). New curricula and programs require different kinds of relationships with communities, different forms of pedagogy, and so on. The balance among the four may vary from school to school or district to district, depending on the current situation, but in the end, every school will have to tackle all four to achieve ambitious goals.

Australian literacy expert and former government leader, Allan Luke, put it this way:

> High schools are more complex, bureaucratic, hierarchical institutions than primary schools and hence more difficult to mobilize and change for improved student outcomes. The task is complex: building and maintaining school ethos, ethics of care, overall professional capacity, counseling and community relations while working with specific curriculum areas to build field-specific pedagogical and curriculum-planning expertise. In any complex organization, leadership, then, doesn't entail a "quick fix" but rather a complex balancing act of coordinating development and improvement of different areas within the school. (Personal communication, May 2011)

An important consideration is the balance among initiatives. On the one hand, many reform efforts suffer from too many separate initiatives. This is especially a problem in secondary schools. Many high schools have multiple initiatives going on at the same time but typically with little or no connection among them or to any overall plan for improvement. It is one way that schools deal with competing internal ideas and interests—by giving everyone something but with no overall resulting effect. Such an approach is distracting for everyone and cannot lead to real progress.

At the same time, some duplication of effort is not necessarily a bad thing, especially in a large school or system. For example, there can be a variety of ways to work on community relationships, several of which can be pursued simultaneously provided that there is awareness of the various approaches and some consistency among them. Similarly, improving teaching in most high schools will require more than one initiative to take into account differing contexts and needs. Getting the balance right between multiple efforts and coherence is a main task of leadership—explaining to everyone in the organization what the components are and how they fit together or, to put it another way, creating the narrative or storyline for what the school or system is doing. The four areas of strategy can serve as that storyline, connecting various initiatives into a coherent whole.

Many reform efforts underestimate the degree to which improving schooling requires the development of particular technical skills, especially those related to effective teaching. One of the serious shortcomings in many reform proposals is the lack of attention given to the specific things that teachers and students should do. Instead, proposals generally favor a focus on motivation or collective learning. The "what" of that learning is often ignored, yet the heart of education is in the work that students do every day, which means that changing outcomes requires changing those activities.

The skills of teaching and organizing learning are not simple at all. Of course, personal attributes such as caring and energy are important, but if teachers do not know *how* to help students learn to do fractions, write paragraphs, or understand chemical interactions, then all the goodwill, data, and accountability in the world will not help very much. This is just one of many places where reforms fall short by focusing on everything but actual teaching and learning practices. A whole chapter in this book is dedicated to changing teaching and learning processes in secondary schools.

The same need applies to schools and systems. Calling for "effective leadership" is all very well, but if leaders do not know how to organize their schools to promote ongoing improvement or how to lead discussions about student work or if systems are not in place to ensure that effective practices become routines, then no amount of rhetoric and commitment to good outcomes will generate the desired results.

One important area in which more effective skills are needed is special education. High schools often have large numbers of students in special education programs. These students are at high risk of not graduating, but there is virtually no discussion in the literature on high school policy about how to provide more effective education for them. Highly successful countries tend to have smaller numbers of students in special education. Yet improving special education services and outcomes requires careful attention to teaching strategies, to the organization of resources, and to systems that prevent students from falling too far behind in the first place.

Consistent effort sustained over time is also vital. Too many teachers have experienced the reform of the year over and over as an initiative is started with great fanfare, only to be abandoned a short time later and replaced by something else new. School improvement does not take place in a month or a year, though important steps can be taken in a year. It requires several years of sustained effort on a consistent strategy.

Finally, there has to be alignment between schools and the district or larger system. This does not mean that every school must do exactly the same things in the same way. An enforced uniformity can be highly dispiriting to people, and ideas have to be adapted to meet the circumstances of different schools. It does mean, though, that the overall approach must be consistent and that other ancillary responsibilities in both schools and districts are matched to and supportive of the main improvement strategies. More will be said on these points in the chapter on implementation.

Part of this consistency and alignment is that every school, not just those considered low performing, must be involved in improvement if systemwide or national goals are to be met.

KNOW THE STATUS AND PROGRESS OF EVERY STUDENT, KNOW THE REASONS FOR ANY PROBLEMS, AND INTERVENE AS SOON AS THERE ARE SIGNS OF DIFFICULTIES

Students say over and over again that the most important factor in deciding whether they come to school, stay in school, or leave school is whether anyone in that institution knows who they are and cares about what happens to them. This is one of the clearest findings in all the research on secondary education.

Yet most high schools are simply not organized to do the work of looking after their students. Even where efforts are made, quite often "caring for" or connecting with students is translated into single strategies such as smaller schools or teacher-advisor systems. Both of these can be helpful but are insufficient. The actions schools need to take in this area include developing personal relationships but go well beyond simply that. The key is to ensure that caring about students is built into the schools' work by having processes in place to ensure that each student's progress is tracked and that there is effective intervention as soon as a student encounters difficulties. "We care about you" only becomes real when it turns into real action to help students overcome their challenges and achieve success and when success for students is the very core of what schools believe they are doing and how their work is organized.

This strategy is listed first because, in my view, it is the easiest to implement and it can pay large dividends very quickly. When students sense the adults really do care, they will often meet us more than half way by increasing their own effort. Moreover, creating these connections and systems is generally consistent with what teachers believe and does not ask for significant changes in daily teaching practice.

At the same time, as soon as one starts delving into the reasons students are not doing well, the other strategies come into play since students' problems involve the courses available, the timetable, school rules, teaching methods, and assessment practices, as well as family and community connections—all of which fall under the other strategies. Often, though, it is easier to get people engaged with these other requirements if one starts with the situations and needs of specific students.

PROVIDE A PROGRAM THAT ENABLES ALL STUDENTS TO ACHIEVE A GOOD OUTCOME

Secondary schools have often taken the position that greater student success is largely a matter of providing enough different courses. If students don't like or are not successful in traditional courses, then we should offer them other courses or programs. Too often, however, this approach has had the wrong consequences. It segregates lower-achieving students through program choices and put them into courses that have low levels of intellectual demand and do not lead either to postsecondary education or to real and meaningful employment. Students soon get the idea that they do not need to do any work because the school does not believe they have much ability. Students in these programs, who in many ways need the best teaching, are often assigned less-experienced teachers.

Instead of this approach, I introduce in this chapter a set of principles to inform program design in high schools no matter who the students are. These principles include the following:

- High expectations
- Open futures—school programs must build in flexibility and support students' later changes of plans
- Credentials that have real value either for further education, employment, or both
- Recovery options so that poor decisions or actions can be remedied and more ambitious pathways pursued
- Self-direction that helps students take responsibility for their own lives
- Whole-school programming that recognizes the importance of the co-curriculum
- Partnerships with other organizations and agencies

These principles do not specify using any particular set of courses or programs. They can apply to many designs and when applied, they vastly increase the chances that students will be motivated to succeed as well as have good opportunities for learning and success. They also reduce the chances that students are assigned to courses that neither they nor their teachers believe have much value.

IMPROVING DAILY TEACHING AND LEARNING IS ESSENTIAL TO ACHIEVING BETTER HIGH SCHOOL OUTCOMES; TO DO THIS REQUIRES A THOUGHTFUL AND SPECIFIC STRATEGY

All institutions struggle with the challenge of staying focused on their real goals in the face of all the daily work and routines.

The core business of high schools is supporting students' learning, yet so much attention inevitably goes to other issues—safety and discipline, staffing, community relations, extracurricular activities, and so on—that schools and districts can easily find themselves giving very little attention to students' learning experiences.

In high schools, this problem is exacerbated by the division into subjects and departments; students often see little coherence across subjects in terms of activities, intellectual demands, and even ways of working. The result can be a student experience that is both difficult and disengaging, which causes school to feel like a series of disconnected and not very purposeful activities—a far cry from what good education should be.

It is hard to get a large high school focused on improving common teaching and learning practices. However, there are some promising routes to doing so. The most important potential avenue is through student assessment practices because these are such powerful drivers of what both teacher and students do every day. The point is not assessment itself but to use assessment as a means of looking at teaching practice. Collective work designed by teachers looking at assessment practices has the potential to be a powerful tool for better schooling by focusing staff on the work students are doing, by changing the kinds of work students are asked to do, and by increasing consistency of student experience across the school.

Another opportunity lies in engaging students more in the daily practices in their classrooms by increasing their voice and input in such areas as the organization of classes and the kinds of work they do. Student voice is an important correlate of student engagement, which is in turn an important correlate of better outcomes. Student voice is also a potentially effective way of changing teaching practice.

A third strategy involves increasing opportunities for independent work by students. Whether in everyday courses or through other venues, including online courses, independent learning can be highly motivating for students and very consistent with the lifelong skills they will need as long as the school actively supports and monitors their progress.

CONNECT SCHOOLS DEEPLY TO THEIR LOCAL AND BROADER COMMUNITY

Schools are necessarily influenced by their communities because students are so highly influenced by their families, peers, neighborhoods, and other associations outside the school. While educators are very aware of this fact, few high schools have strong outreach programs to interact with these broader communities. Moreover, schools often see communities primarily as sources of bad influences rather than looking for the resources and strengths that even the most stressed communities have. Parents and families can, of course, present challenges and difficulties, but they are also vital not only in supporting students but also to providing a supportive environment for the work of the school. With some care and effort, the natural tensions between schools and families can be managed.

Communities are also sources of learning for students, if schools are willing to use them in that way. Both employers and postsecondary institutions have considerable potential for increasing the range of learning spaces and opportunities for students and for providing different models and horizons for students in difficult circumstances. The part-time work that many students do provides another opportunity for learning instead of being seen, as it often is, as a distraction from students' schoolwork.

As with any other area of work in a school, these community connections do not come without effort. Someone has to do the work of initiating, organizing, and maintaining the relationships between the schools and the community. In many schools this is the kind of task that is not assigned to anyone, so it tends not to get done. However, the rewards in terms of increased trust, increased understanding, and new ways to connect with students are very valuable and well worth the effort.

RESOURCING IMPROVEMENT

A first reaction to all these ideas might be to ask how they can be managed in a time of tight resources. While more is said on this point in Chapter 7, it is important to think about how much money is currently wasted in our schools as a result of failure.

Consider that in most English-speaking countries, up to 30% of students are not completing secondary education in a timely way. This is certainly a human tragedy, but it also represents a very large waste of resources. If 30% of students take at least one extra year of high school, and some portion of those take two or more extra years (many of whom still do not graduate), then the cost of secondary education is dramatically increased from what it would be if those students graduated on time, even with significant additional help. When one factors in students who fail or withdraw from a course but still graduate, the cost is even higher. For example, the province of Ontario spends approximately $6 billion on high schools each year for some 600,000 students, or about $10,000 per student per year. Even after subtracting fixed costs, the additional cost of reteaching the tens of thousands of students who have failed must certainly be in the hundreds of millions of dollars. What if those resources were redeployed to helping students succeed in the first place instead of being spent on their retaking classes, courses, and years of study? It is highly likely that we could generate significantly more success while also spending significantly less money.

There is a further reason why a reduction in failures should be a primary goal of every school: the widely acknowledged finding, not just in education but also in psychology, that failure generally tends to depress future effort. It may be widely believed that failing is "good for you" because it teaches important life lessons, but the empirical evidence of many years does not support that belief. As one instance, consider how strong the relationship is between students' failing a year in elementary school or even one course in their first year of high school and failing to graduate from high school (Allensworth & Easton, 2007; Rumberger & Lim, 2008). For most of these students, failure was not a spur to greater effort but the opposite.

CONCLUSION

This chapter provides an overview of a four-part comprehensive strategy for improving high schools and increasing the proportion of students who graduate. The strategy is ambitious but feasible in ordinary schools, with regular folks doing regular jobs. It requires focus and persistence but not superhuman people or effort.

The remaining chapters describe each of the four main strategies in detail.

Take-Aways

- Improving high school outcomes requires attention to four key points:

  1. Know the status and progress of every student, know the reasons for any problems, and intervene as soon as there are signs of difficulties.

  2. Provide a program that enables all students to achieve a good outcome.

  3. Improving daily teaching and learning is essential to achieving better high school outcomes; to do this requires a thoughtful and specific strategy.

  4. Connect schools deeply to their local and broader community.

- Lasting improvement requires sustained effort from many people over years.

- Improvement requires changes in what people actually do every day, which in turn means that people have to learn new skills and habits. It's about behavior and action not just ideas and beliefs.

- Improving student success can free significant resources that can be used to support students rather than to reteach courses.

CHAPTER THREE

Connecting With Every Student

Two teachers in adjacent rooms begin their 10th-grade mathematics course. Each is teaching a group of struggling students. The first teacher starts by telling students, "This is a tough course, and if you do not work hard from the very beginning you will fail, as have many students before you." The second teacher starts by telling the students that they are all going to pass the course. How does he know that? Two reasons: "First, I am a great teacher. Second, I've had way worse students than you and they all passed." Now imagine the responses of these students and how these very first sentences set up their expectations and behavior.

This chapter discusses what schools and systems can and need to do to ensure that every student is known by staff, that every student has a sense of belonging in the school, and that schools have systems in place to identify emerging problems in student progress and can intervene early to prevent failure and disengagement. The shorthand phrase for all of this is "connecting with every student" or "caring."

In 2004, Ontario as a province did not report a provincial high school graduation rate to the national data agency, Statistics Canada. Simply put, the system did not know with any accuracy what proportion of its students were completing high school, either in the normal four years or after longer periods of time. By 2007, every school, district, and the province as a whole not only knew how many students were graduating but also knew how many and which students were gaining all their expected credits in each year of high school and so were on track to graduate. Moreover, every school has a process for identifying students who are off track and takes steps to help them get back on the path to graduation.

This chapter is first of four main chapters on creating strategies for more graduates because the most important single shift that a secondary school or system can make if it wants to improve outcomes can be stated in one sentence: "Know the status and progress of every student, know the reasons for any problems, and intervene as soon as there are signs of difficulties."

This idea is so central that I am going to repeat it:

Know the status and progress of every student, know the reasons for any problems, and intervene as soon as there are signs of difficulties.

Research findings going back years (Balfanz, Bridgeland, Moore, & Fox, 2010; Bridgeland, Dilulio, & Morison, 2006; Mac Iver & Mac Iver, 2009) have alerted us to the importance of strong personal connections between schools and students. Indeed, the single most important factor identified by students for keeping them in school is the sense that somebody at the school actually cared about them as people. Before launching Ontario's drive to improve high school graduation rates in 2005, the ministry of education commissioned researchers at the Hospital for Sick Children in Toronto to gather information about why students had left secondary schools before graduating (Ferguson, Tilleczek, Boydell, & Rummens, 2005). They heard very consistent messages from students; here are a few of the many they report:

Maybe [I would have stayed] if they actually tried to help me. They never did; they just kicked me out or gave me detentions or . . . expelled me. Nobody actually lifted a finger.

I went to my guidance counselor . . . she told me "You know, the best thing for you since [you] have so much trouble with school . . . is to probably drop out of school now, [be]cause now is the time for you to do it." . . . when she told me this, I was shocked because she is the guidance counselor. They are the people who are supposed to encourage you to stay in school, not to drop out.

I was never disrespectful to teachers or anything but a lot of teachers were disrespectful towards students.

I was having trouble with the teachers and principal at school. And it just bothered me so much that I didn't feel like going anymore.

Many occasions in my own experience reinforce that connection. As deputy minister in Ontario, I visited many high schools. I vividly remember a young woman at one school talking about how, in 10th grade, she was not attending high school, failing her classes, taking drugs, and in trouble with police. But, she said, there was a guidance counselor at the school who simply "would not let go of me." Two years later, she was on track to graduate, out of drugs, no longer in legal trouble, and had a whole new attitude and faith in her ability thanks largely, she said, to that single teacher's faith in her.

Another time, I visited an alternative school in a small community. One of the teachers had gone through the school's roster and identified all students who needed only a few more credits to graduate but who had not reenrolled that fall. Mr. Mac (as the students called him) called every one of those students and told them he was starting a program for them and wanted them to be there. More than 20 showed up and well into the year, 90% of them were back on track to graduate. As one very large young man told me, "I knew I needed to graduate, but I was not going to go back to that school. Mr. Mac gave me an option that has saved my life."

There are thousands of such stories in secondary schools around the world. Connecting with students is hardly a new idea. Much writing about schools talks about the importance of caring. Many efforts have been made to address this issue through, for example, the small-schools movement funded by the Gates Foundation, the creation of schools-within-schools, teacher-advisor systems, or similar programs. But those efforts were not enough, as the Gates Foundation concluded based on the evaluations of its small schools efforts (American Institutes for Research and SRI International, 2006).

Creating smaller schools or schools-within-schools was not enough because the requirement to "know the status and progress of every student, know the reasons for any problems, and intervene as soon as there are signs of difficulties" is about more than a structure and a caring attitude. Success requires a set of systems and attitudes that have to be built and sustained across an entire school and system. Caring has to turn into action that helps students be and stay successful. The important thing is not a specific program model, since no single model is likely to work with all students, but the existence in the whole school of organized methods of knowing students, monitoring their progress, and intervening early. All three elements are necessary, but there are many possible ways of organizing each one.

In practical terms, caring is demonstrated in a school or system by the following:

- There is at least one staff member (and usually more than one) who knows something about each student—her or his character, family background, orientation toward learning, life outside the school, educational history, interests, and personal challenges.
- The school knows the current academic status of all students, including course choice and progress in those courses.
- An organized system is in place to identify all students who are struggling in a course.
- An organized process of intervention takes place when a student is identified as struggling.
- There are various mechanisms to help students get back on track toward on-time graduation.

When all of these elements are in place, students are more likely to feel like a part of the school and the school is likely to experience reductions in failure rates and discipline problems.

MONITORING STUDENT PROGRESS

There are many ways schools can organize themselves to achieve this goal. Consider the way that Ontario tried to address this challenge:

First, each high school in the province created a "student success leadership team," which was responsible for monitoring student progress. It was usually led by the principal (but sometimes by a vice principal) and normally included several other key staff members, such as guidance counselors, student success teachers, or department heads. These teams met regularly to discuss the school's progress toward helping more students succeed. They looked at data, evaluated current efforts, and considered what other steps might be useful. This team regularly reviewed the progress of all students and discussed what could be done for those students who were struggling—before they failed! Typically, the team looked at any students who seemed to be at risk of failing a course or where teachers or other staff members were reporting a concern such as poor attendance or a negative attitude. In most schools this is not a huge task because most students are progressing reasonably. Furthermore, when this kind of monitoring becomes a regular feature of the way the school works, the team gets to know students better or makes sure that someone in the school does.

Typically, the monitoring process leads to some further discussion of students' difficulties. Someone on staff talks with each student to find out what the problem is. Sometimes they are academic problems, sometimes they are caused by personality conflicts with particular teachers, or sometimes they are related to things in the student's life outside of school. The review process is a structured way to ensure that the school is aware of what is happening in each case.

Reviewing student status is not the point, however. The review process has to lead to effective intervention. Someone has to follow up and find out why a student is off track and what can be done about it and then action must be taken to help the student.

Sometimes students are not graduating for reasons that turn out to be quite minor. One Ontario high school found that it had 40 students who had met all the graduation requirements except that, for various reasons, they had not completed the requirement for 40 hours of volunteer work. This was quickly remedied and all 40 students were added to the graduation list. In other cases, students may be short one course or even only part of one course, which is another situation that can usually be remedied fairly easily. Another example would be students who missed a substantial part of a course due to illness or family issues. Quite often, these problems can be resolved with a little discussion between the student, the teacher, and another staff member who can help broker a solution. Many schools found that once they started looking at what was preventing students from graduating, they could increase their graduation numbers substantially without enormous effort.

Of course, this is not always the case. Some students have serious problems. But quite a bit of evidence suggests that for many students, small interventions can matter. It seems that in many cases, as little as 20 to 30 minutes of supportive adult attention can move a student from the wrong path to the right one (Levin, 2009). Susan Nolen, a professor at the University of Washington, asks teachers working with her to spend 30 minutes outside of class just getting to know a student with whom they do not relate very well. Ray Wlodkowski (1983), a U.S. researcher, has something similar he calls a "two by 10" strategy, in which for two minutes a day for 10 consecutive days, a teacher has a personal conversation with a difficult or challenging student about something of interest to the student. Both researchers report that these simple steps not only give teachers a deeper and more positive understanding of the students but also often dramatically alter the way the students engage in their classes. Moreover, they communicate a powerful message to students— that the school is always interested in helping them get on the path to success.

ASSIGNING RESPONSIBILITY FOR FOLLOWING STUDENTS

Who does this work in a school? Many high schools consider this the job of guidance counselors and many guidance counselors do this work well, but it cannot be left to counselors alone for several reasons. First, there aren't enough counselors. In many schools, there is one guidance counselor for every 400 or 500 students. That simply isn't sufficient even in a high school with quite high success rates.

Second, counselors have quite a few other responsibilities. In many schools, their time is largely taken up with providing advice to students on course selection or on postsecondary education. They may have responsibilities for various administrative tasks such as working with social service agencies or other community groups. The time they have available is not usually going to be sufficient.

Third, the most important part of this support and advocacy function is the connection a student feels with a particular staff member. Because students differ greatly, they will not all feel that connection with the same teachers. Some students may prefer a teacher of the same gender or ethnic background. Some are shy and need someone quiet while others are vocal and need someone strong and outgoing. Similarly, staff members will have different abilities or interests in connecting with different students. One of the reasons that assigned teacher-advisor systems sometimes fail is that they do not take into account individual preferences for personal connections. It is important to respect these affinities. If every student is to form at least one meaningful connection with an adult, then many, if not all, of the professional staff—and often some of the support staff—will have to be involved. Let's remember that the key is to consider every student, not just to identify a supposed high-risk group and focus on them, since that will inevitably miss some students.

Connecting with students in this way raises the very delicate issue of advocating for them with other staff. It is essential that teachers be able to have conversations with other teachers about the individual students with whom they are working. Consider a staff member talking with a student who has stopped attending and doing work in one of his courses. The student reports feeling that another teacher is not really interested in him or perhaps he feels another teacher is picking on him. The staff person, upon hearing this comment, must be able to take this concern up with the teacher in question. It is not a matter of making demands or assigning blame but of investigating the nature and source of a problem so that it can be resolved. Is there something that that teacher can do to make the student feel included so that he or she returns to class and completes the course?

In many schools, social norms among staff prohibit such conversations, which is not only a detriment to students but also to teachers who may discover through such conversations ways that they could improve their teaching and increase their success. After all, we all have behaviors that have effects on others that we neither intend nor are aware of; the only way to improve is to get honest feedback on our behavior. This is what good professional colleagues do for each other, but it is all too infrequent in most organizations, including most schools.

The reality is that every teacher will have some encounters with students who do not appreciate her or his style or approach. It's inevitable. The key is to remove blame from the discussion and not to focus on anyone's shortcomings (since we all have plenty of them) but on what might be done to improve a situation to the benefit of students.

It is the task of the school leadership to foster this kind of open and positive feedback among staff (and with students and the wider community as well, which I will discuss more later). This means that school leadership teams have to create the norms that make meaningful feedback not just possible but normal or expected, including feedback to leaders on their behavior and its effects. Staff members need to discuss these expectations openly, figure out how to make them work, share their misgivings, and work collectively toward a more open setting. Although this seems a daunting task, there is lots of advice on ways to have those difficult conversations (e.g., Singleton & Linton, 2005). The upside is that all of us really do want to know what others think about us and even if sometimes that knowledge disappoints us, it also gives us the opportunity to do better in future.

One of the elements of the Ontario strategy that was specifically intended to address this need was the creation of "student success teachers." As part of the collective agreements with secondary teachers in Ontario in 2005, the ministry of education agreed to fund an additional staff position in each secondary school, to be called a "student success teacher" (SST). The job of these teachers can be described colloquially as "to look after students who needed but were not getting the right attention."

The SSTs take on this role in different ways in different schools. In all schools, they are part of the school's "student success leadership team" and therefore deeply connected to the school's overall improvement strategy. Sometimes they teach particular courses or look after *credit recovery* and *credit rescue* programs (described in the next chapter). They often gather information about the situations and problems of particular students so that they can help the school find better ways to work with those students. They liaise closely in most schools with guidance staff to ensure they are not duplicating work. They act as advocates for students with other staff and, because this is known to be part of their job, are often able to do so more readily than other staff might. In every school, they provide an additional pair of hands and a mind and heart focused on helping students be successful and are therefore usually a key part of creating the right overall climate in a school.

While attention to individual students is vital, it is also important to look at patterns of success and failure within a school or system. Teams looking at student progress in an organized and methodical way using data on failures, marks, attendance, and so on often start to identify common factors affecting many students that had not been noticed before. An example would be particular courses that are causing the most difficulty for the most students. Sometimes this is a matter of whether a particular course is offered in first or second semester or at a particular time of day. For example, if students put all their compulsory or most difficult courses in the same semester they may find themselves struggling, whereas if they had a more even distribution of different kinds of courses it would make their workload more manageable and might also improve their motivation. Sometimes these analyses suggest work with a department or a teacher on course requirements to make sure these are consistent with other courses. Most schools are unaware of these patterns, but once they start looking, they are able to find areas in which, again, some fairly simple steps can be taken to create large benefits for students.

One of the most interesting examples of monitoring student progress has been developed in the United Kingdom and is shown in Figure 3.1. Each figure is 1% of the student population in a school, course, or grade, and each color represents a different status. The picture overall gives an immediate picture of how many students are facing which kinds of challenges and is a powerful visual way to express progress. Of course, the specific codes matched to the colors can be adapted to any set of issues of interest to a school or system.

Sue Hackman, Chief Advisor on School Standards in England, put it as follows:

> You can always tell if the data is a great lever because a teacher will respond to it by asking a useful question such as "How do they do that?" or "Which of my students does that apply to?" (Personal communication, May, 2011)

Figure 3.1   Stickmen Figure for Student Progress in the United Kingdom

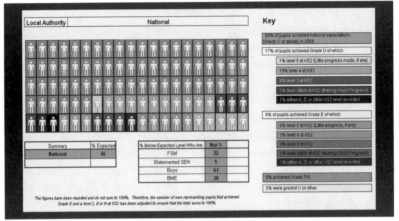

SOURCE: Used with permission, UK Department of Education.

Student success teams keep issues of student success and graduation on the school's agenda constantly. They make sure that the whole staff discusses these issues regularly, that these issues are part of professional development work, that all staff members are aware of the data, and that there is ongoing focus on the school's improvement agenda.

PAYING ATTENTION TO SPECIFIC GROUPS

It is particularly important to get to know and track students in their first year of secondary school. If students get off track in their very first year or semester, then their chances of graduating drop dramatically, so schools need to take some special measures for their new students.

One valuable option is to build links with the "feeder" schools that provide students to a high school. In successful systems, leaders and staff in high schools know and work with leaders and staff in junior high or middle schools. Teachers talk about their expectations for students' work and behavior across the two organizations. Exchanges across schools about curriculum expectations and teaching practices allow secondary teachers to have a better idea of what new students are used to. Sharing information about students can also be useful to teachers in secondary schools, as it allows them to have a better idea of what to expect, though one always has to be cautious not to let previous performance shape future expectations. For many students, high school looms as a scary place, so inviting students and parents to visit the high school in the year prior to the students' enrollment there can be helpful. Teachers need to be especially attentive to their freshmen in the first few weeks of class and the school should have a system in place to alert staff when a new student appears to be struggling, even in the first month of classes.

Some schools have also used various "buddy" systems in which new students are paired with older students to ease their transition. For instance, one school has a process in which junior high and high school teachers jointly discuss the characteristics of new students and find appropriate buddies. The high school often matches new students who are most at risk with some of their top juniors and seniors; the chances of bullying drop dramatically when a new student has an immediate pal in, say, a top athlete in the school.

The same concern should apply to new students entering the school who are not freshmen. The first few weeks or months in a new setting are critical and need careful monitoring. There is evidence that students who change schools frequently are less likely to graduate. The reasons for this seem obvious: more mobility is often connected with greater poverty and less family stability, both of which are negative factors for school success. But it is also the case that students who change schools are less known to staff and so are less likely to get the attention they may need to resolve problems.

Proactive steps can be taken to try to give new students a sense of belonging, including ensuring that each new student is given some connection with staff and other students. If schools think of each new student, whatever age or grade, as requiring some of the same attention as freshmen, they will be on the way to more success with this group.

Getting students off to a strong start is important, but equally important is the idea that we should not give up on students later. Students who are in 11th or 12th grade are still only 17 or 18 years old. Their lives are still in front of them, and it is well worth a significant adult investment to improve their prospects for the next 50, 60, or even 70 years. A large number of students who do not complete high school in the normal three or four years stay enrolled in an effort to graduate. However, success rates in this extra year are quite low. In the Canadian provinces of Ontario and Alberta, only about a quarter of the students who return for an extra year actually graduate, which is both disappointing and expensive.

Clearly, there is a significant opportunity here to improve graduation rates, since most of these students are close to meeting graduation requirements. Yet few schools or systems think systematically about this group and how they could best be served. Indeed, many schools have no idea how many such students they have, who they are, or what their requirements are for graduation. Reaching out to returning students, paying special attention to their timetables and assigned teachers, and connecting them to advocates in the school are all steps that will help more of these students graduate.

Schools need to pay specific attention to students who show strong ability but are disaffected. Most high schools have some students of this kind; they have all the ability necessary to do the work but have decided not to make the effort. A range of factors can create this situation, from feelings of boredom to resistance to the many rules of most high schools to personal problems of various kinds. Sometimes these students are especially challenging because they are bright and rebellious—which, it must be said, is not an uncommon combination in teenagers. As always, the first step is for someone to know the students and their concerns followed by efforts to find a way to engage them in meeting the requirements for graduation. Independent learning options, discussed more in later chapters, are sometimes particularly promising for these students, many of whom may chafe at the behavioral restrictions of many high schools.

Another important element of connecting occurs when students leave the school without graduating. Despite the best efforts of a school, there will be some students who end up leaving. Time and time again students have said that they wanted to return but did not feel able to go back to the school they had left, which was often not under the best of circumstances. Schools can make deliberate efforts to ensure that students know they are welcome to return when they feel ready. It is possible to say, "Things are not working well at this moment and you may feel that you need to do something else right now, but we want you to know that when you feel ready to return, we will welcome you back with a clean slate." This is an important message to communicate even though it may feel difficult at the time. At the same time, students leaving without graduating should never feel that this is something that the school has encouraged or is happy to see; the first (and second and third and fourth . . .) effort must always be to help students succeed, not to send them away.

ATTENDANCE, DISCIPLINE, AND SUSPENSIONS

Rules and disciplinary issues are often areas of substantial conflict in high schools. High schools are caught in a situation in which they are responsible for student safety while also dealing with young people who increasingly feel themselves to be—and are—close to adulthood and who may resent what they perceive as excessive control on their behavior. Especially in high-poverty schools, concerns for safety and the management of large numbers of students can lead to highly regulated settings, from strict controls on who can be where at any given time to the presence of police, metal detectors, and constantly locked doors. Just at the age when adolescents want and need to experience increased independence, schools may give them less autonomy than they had in the elementary years. As one teacher put it, "These kids have jobs where they are expected to work with customers, handle money, open or close the business, and make important decisions. Then they come to school and we won't let them go to the toilet without a pass. No wonder they don't like it!"

These issues are tricky because the pressures on schools about safety and discipline are very real. Even though schools are generally safer places for young people than the neighborhoods around them, public expectations for safety of young people in schools are very high. Safety incidents in schools get vastly disproportionate public and media attention for reasons that are easy to understand if not necessarily sound. No school can ignore these issues, but there is a fine line between what is necessary for student safety and situations that foster student disaffection.

The most common place where these tensions play out in secondary schools is in issues concerning attendance. Teachers overwhelmingly feel that attendance is not only fundamental to learning but that it is also a sign of student commitment, so not attending is seen as disrespectful as well as damaging to academic achievement. In many high schools, debates about how to improve attendance—often framed as setting consequences for absence—are among the most frequent topics of staff discussion.

Quite a bit of evidence shows that attendance is correlated with student achievement. The question is whether poor attendance is the cause of problems or the result of them. While there is inevitably going to be some of each, the argument here is that low attendance is often more a reflection of problems than a cause and that the solution to poor attendance does not primarily lie in rules concerning attendance but in creating a positive and inviting school setting where students want to be—and not only to see their friends. It is easy to investigate this question empirically in a school by examining patterns of attendance; for example, there may be a pattern in which some students are problematic attendees in all their classes, while others only miss some classes. I had direct experience with a student who, in her last year of high school, was very frequently late for her first class in the morning. When I talked to her about it, she made it clear that this was her way of showing her lack of respect for that teacher; in her other classes and in her second-term morning class, she had no attendance issue.

One instance of how attendance is linked to instruction lies in the potential impact of grading practices on attendance. A student who gets off to a bad start in a course may realize that because the grading policy averages all grades for the course, her or his chances of doing well in the course are very low after only a few weeks. This is an invitation to stop attending. It is also an example of how an intervention from a staff member could result in the student and teacher coming to an agreement on how the student could still have a chance to do reasonably well in the course. It is possible to move from a negative to a positive situation if an opportunity is provided for the student to recover the lost marks so as to be able to succeed in the course. Without an early warning system and a system of interventions, large numbers of students can end up missing classes and credits for just this reason.

It is also important for adults to separate their egos from how they judge student behavior and not to confuse attendance with achievement. Sometimes teachers see poor attendance as a lack of respect for them personally. This is sometimes what students intend, as in the case just mentioned, but more often students' choices have much more to do with their lives than with their views about those teaching them. One only has to think back to one's own high school days to realize how little consideration most students give to their teachers as people.

The point behind these comments is to avoid the tendency to want to punish students for missing classes. From a human standpoint that desire is entirely understandable, but from an educational standpoint it is entirely misguided because it usually misses the point of why students are not attending and because punishment, as shown by a very large amount of research, is not an effective way to change people's behavior (for a recent review, see Lipsey, 2009).

This is not to suggest that teachers or schools should ignore poor attendance. Poor attendance is clearly a sign that something is wrong and needs to be investigated. The proposals in this chapter would make that an automatic practice. Schools should make it clear that students are expected to attend. However, the first emphasis must always be on the expectation for achievement; attendance without achievement is of no benefit to anyone, whereas achievement without attendance, while annoying to some adults, is still achievement and should be recognized as such. The central message, in other words, is always about wanting students to achieve. Everything else students do should be seen in light of whether they are learning and developing appropriately.

This brings us to the issue of discipline. Schools require a reasonable amount of order and decorum and they must—they truly must—be felt to be safe places by all who inhabit them, both by adults and young people. Because of the natural tendency of young people to be rebellious and their need to differentiate themselves from adults, high schools will always be places where there are behavioral issues ranging from mild to very serious.

As is the case for attendance, discipline problems tend to take up vast amounts of time, especially for school administrators. They cannot be avoided but they, too, must be seen through the lens of what is most likely to get students back on track. Educators' responsibilities are different from those of other positions. If we see a neighbor doing something illegal, our response might be to call the police. If we see a student doing something wrong, though, our first thought should be how we can use this as an educational moment to try to affect that student's understanding and future behavior in a positive way. As with safety issues, legal concerns and public scrutiny can push schools toward a stronger punishment orientation when sound educational thinking might push them toward something more forgiving and educational. Nobody should interpret that stance to mean that that there should be no consequences for student misbehavior or that schools should ignore or condone wrong behavior. Quite the opposite: schools should be places with very high expectations for the behavior of everyone in them. The difference is not in the expectations, it is in the understanding of what counts as an educative response.

This need is even more important because of the very strong evidence that various forms of punishment in schools are systematically related to students' gender, ethnicity, or other such characteristics. Many studies have shown that male and some minority students are more likely to be subject to formal discipline, such as suspension, than are other students (e.g., Gregory & Weinstein, 2008). Moreover, some students receive harsher treatment than others for the same offense on the basis of color or social status rather than prior behavior. In other words, justice practices in schools, as in the larger society, show signs of systemic discrimination. Since the students most likely to be subject to this are precisely those students at high risk of not graduating, the school as an educational institution has to consider carefully how it can balance its requirements for order with its educational responsibilities and commitment to equity.

There are alternatives to the usual forms of discipline. Many schools have been able to dramatically reduce not just suspensions but also—and more important—the disciplinary incidents that gave rise to them by adopting various kinds of dispute resolution and restorative justice processes. Restorative justice puts

Fletcher's Meadows High School

With an enrollment more than 50% above its capacity and a highly diverse student population (60% Caribbean Canadian and 30% South Asian), Fletcher's Meadows High School in Brampton, Ontario, was facing serious behavioral issues (including bullying) at the start of 2009. To address these problems, the school adopted a multipart strategy:

a. Maintaining an excellent learning program and environment, which included theme-based interdisciplinary programs during the year as well as summer and after-school programs, a credit recovery program, two specialist high skills majors, and dual credits

b. Establishing an outstanding extracurricular program

c. Creating opportunities for student voice and leadership, including peer mediation

d. Hiring a diverse staff and providing training in equity and inclusive education, progressive discipline and restorative practices, and bullying prevention

e. Developing strong parental involvement

f. Establishing an array of community partnerships with local agencies, community groups, parks and recreation, the police, and local businesses

As a result, academic achievement improved, behavior improved, attendance improved, and the number of suspensions fell by 30% in one year.

the focus on how to repair harm others have caused (see www .restorativejustice.org). There is also a strong relationship between students' sense of the school as a caring and engaging place and their behavior. Improved teaching practices and greater student engagement in classrooms and the school as a whole are among the most effective ways of reducing behavior problems.

STUDENT VOICE

A further important component of connecting with students concerns the role that students play in their own schooling.

There is an understandable tendency in the education policy world to talk about schooling as something we do to students or to sometimes refer to students as if they were raw materials in a production process. That is a misleading analogy; in reality, learning is mainly something students do by and for themselves. To be sure, there is much input and guidance from others involved, but in the end students must construct their own knowledge, their own understanding, and their own way of being in the world.

Students' sense of motivation and engagement with their schooling is a very powerful influence on their outcomes. While some of this surely comes from students' backgrounds, homes, and personalities, there is also much that schools can do to build more student engagement and commitment by giving students a more active role—a voice—in many aspects of their schooling.

Many studies have shown that large numbers of high school students are bored by their schooling. A recent Canadian study (Canadian Education Association, 2009) of students from sixth through 12th grade found that fewer than half reported being intellectually engaged in their English or mathematics classes. The National Research Council (NRC, 2003) in the United States reported that "40% to 60% of high school students are chronically disengaged; they are inattentive, exert little effort, do not complete tasks, and claim to be bored" (p. 18). In many studies of dropouts, students rate boredom or disengagement as a major contributing factor. Moreover, disengagement tends to increase throughout the later years of schooling (NRC, 2003). And levels of engagement, just like overall school performance, vary a great deal even among schools with very similar demographics (Canadian Education Association, 2009).

It stands to reason then that schools would benefit from getting more feedback from students and finding ways to bring students actively into the education process rather than as passive recipients.

The idea of student voice is hardly new; in the 1960s, students began advocating for more influence in schools. Many examples of interesting initiatives are available (such as the example in the box of the Harris Federation Student Commission in England). Despite this powerful rationale and many examples of successful practices, in most high schools, students do not have an organized, active role in shaping their own learning or the school as an institution.

Engagement itself is not enough, of course. Schools are fundamentally about students' developing skills and knowledge, but it is hard to see how schools can achieve those goals without high levels of engagement, since that is what causes students to make the required efforts. The NRC (2003) report on student engagement cites students' competence and control ("I can"), values and goals ("I want to"), and a sense of belonging ("I belong") as essential elements of student commitment and effort. Schools can help build all of these through various forms of student voice.

Student voice operates at two levels. An important component takes place in classrooms as teachers involve their students in setting goals and standards and organizing learning activities. These ideas are discussed more fully in Chapter 5 on teaching and learning.

A second important approach to student voice happens at the school or district level as students are asked to play a more significant role in shaping the way the schools work. There are many ways in which schools encourage student input on important aspects of the way the school is run. Examples include the following:

- Having students on school improvement teams
- Inviting student input on important policy and program decisions
- Involving students in the school's staff professional development
- Gathering and sharing survey data from students about their feelings and attitudes toward school

Engaging students does not mean only working with the most articulate or top-performing students either. It is especially important to hear from those who are quietest, those who are least successful, and especially those for whom school is the greatest struggle. The very act of asking someone for their viewpoint is the first step toward building trust and commitment. It is important in all work on student voice to find ways to reach a broad cross section of students. Indeed, involving students in designing student voice activities seems an essential first step.

An Example of Student Voice

The Harris Federation (www.harrisfederation.org.uk) is a network of secondary schools in south London, England. Prior to entering the federation, these schools were mainly attended by poor and minority children, and many of them had very poor success records. While the federation does many things to improve student outcomes, one of its most interesting initiatives was the creation of the student commission. Each of the seven schools that were in the federation at that time went through a process of electing student representatives to the commission. Any student could stand for election and all students voted after hearing speeches from those nominated. The 67 students on the commission (at least nine from each school) then went through a series of meetings with principals, staff, and external experts—including some of the top researchers in England—to discuss how the schools could become more engaging and successful places for students. The students found the experience profound; as one said in a conversation, "One thing we learned was how hard good teaching is." The whole process generated a group of student leaders who understood much more about their schools and were committed to working with staff to make these schools even more engaging and effective places. (Harris Learning Commission, 2011)

Many other examples exist as well. The province of Ontario requires elected student representatives to sit on all school boards in the province. These student trustees play an important role in reminding the adults of the views and needs of students. The government of Wales has required students on all school improvement teams and developed a support system for them (www.pupilvoicewales.org.uk). The province of Alberta has a similar initiative to increase student voice (www.speakout.alberta.ca).

Many instruments also exist for gathering student opinion. As one example, *Tell Them From Me* (http://www.thelearningbar.com/ttfm/student-survey.php) is a system for monitoring student views on various school issues using a rolling online survey that can be customized to include issues of interest to a particular school or district. The tool provides schools or systems with ongoing, anonymous feedback from students on issues such as their sense of security, engagement, or intellectual challenge. It allows rapid feedback as well as comparisons over time and among different groups of students.

CONCLUSION

This chapter has focused on the importance of building connections with students, monitoring their progress, and taking action to keep students on track for engagement and success. All of this is a first and essential step to helping more students graduate, but it is not enough. Caring and connection only work when accompanied by the right programs, settings, and practices. We will next turn to curriculum and program structures, which form another essential part of the story.

Take-Aways

- Strong personal connections with every student are the single most important factor in helping students succeed in high school.

- These relationships cannot be left to chance; schools must create the structures and processes to ensure that each student is known and cared for, that each student's progress is being tracked, and that active steps are taken immediately when students are seen to be falling behind.

- In many cases, it only takes a small action to make a very big difference to a student.

- Schools should also look at patterns of student success and failure to determine areas where changes in policy or practice may be needed.

- Although many strategies are generic, some particular groups of students, such as those returning to school after leaving, require specific attention and approaches.

- Good attendance and discipline are more likely to emerge from good relationships and effective pedagogy than vice versa.

- Active engagement of students in creating the right kind of school culture is a powerful strategy.

CHAPTER FOUR

Curriculum and Graduation Requirements

The main difference between elementary schools and high schools is the much greater importance that high schools place on the structure of the curriculum as expressed in courses and graduation requirements. All schools require curriculum content to be meaningful to students and to address essential skills, but in secondary schools this content is turned into courses that students study as specific chunks or elements, with specific pieces required to graduate. This division into subjects was mentioned earlier as one of the elements that make high schools more difficult to change, but it is important to understand more fully the powerful effects of this structure on the way high schools work and on what happens to students. Courses shape what students study, what work they do, and who their teachers are.

While program structures are important, student success is more about teaching than programs. With excellent teaching, students can be interested in and learn in almost any course, but where the quality of teaching is poor, no course will seem very relevant, especially for students who do not have clear life goals and so are not very willing to put up with something now in the hope of getting something later. Course offerings and choices, then, should not be seen as the primary mechanism for addressing students' varying interests or skills. They should be, however, part of any overall strategy to increase graduation rates.

The central problem in high school programming has been trying to construct courses and programs that meet important goals for public education while also accommodating students' varying interests, talents, plans, and abilities and to do so without stratifying students into tracks that lead some students to systematically worse outcomes. The goal must be to provide every student with real opportunities to obtain meaningful skills, knowledge, and credentials—what former Ontario Education Minister Gerard Kennedy referred to as "a good outcome for every student."

Let me repeat that goal also: *The goal of every high school should be to provide a program that enables all students to achieve a good outcome.*

More specifically, the questions to be faced include the following:

- What courses or requirements must be met by all students and which are optional?
- How does the school curriculum accommodate students' many interests, especially those beyond traditional high school subjects?
- How does the school relate to the world of work, given that many students will be working immediately after high school?
- How does the school accommodate some of the needs of particular groups of students?
- What organizational issues are important in curriculum and instruction?

The question of what should be required of students for graduation from high school is not going to be resolved in these pages. After a century of debate, there is still no consensus at all on this issue. Virtually everyone believes there should be at least some common requirements and virtually everyone believes there should be some flexibility or choice, but how much and specifically what should be required or optional is a subject of deep disagreement.

School systems and countries vary quite significantly in how they structure these issues, but their choices do not seem to be related to their ability to help most students graduate; there are highly successful systems that have relatively few electives and others that have a great many. There are successful systems with quite prescriptive curricula and others that give much more discretion to schools and teachers. My own predilection is generally against making too many things compulsory (which applies not only to courses but to rules and processes as well). In general, I believe that the opportunity to make choices builds engagement and commitment. In Ontario, the government did make some modest changes in graduation requirements, such as giving a greater place to cooperative education and recognizing dual credits (discussed more below). For a school or district, however, graduation requirements are typically set externally, so the real issue is not whether the requirements are correct but how to help students succeed under whatever set of requirements they face.

The discussion begins with the fundamental challenge of diversity in course offerings—how to have curriculum that engages students while also meeting the goals of public secondary education. This is, in large part, a discussion of the place of tracks or streams in high school programs, including in particular vocational or technical education. However, no matter which programs are offered, schools need to give attention to organizational issues such as timetables, assigning teachers to courses, and arrangements to promote student success within the program. Of special importance is how schools help students who have missed credits or fallen behind. Another section considers the role of alternative programs or schools and yet another part of the chapter discusses co-curricular programs as a central part of the high school experience.

THE CHALLENGE OF DIVERSE STUDENT INTERESTS

The whole history of secondary education is suffused with conflict between the desire for a common curriculum that prepares all students for community life, further education, and skilled work and on the other hand, the belief that a single curriculum cannot be suited to the highly varied interests and motivation levels of the diverse students in our schools.

The debate has been a vigorous one with different answers holding sway at different historical moments. It is also a debate that is very much influenced by ongoing changes in both postsecondary education and in the labor market. As high school has become a basic requisite for everyone, as the requirements for advanced education have changed, and as the nature of the labor market has changed, so people's ideas about what is required for secondary education have changed.

These developments have been well described elsewhere (e.g., Grubb, 2011; Harvard Graduate School of Education, 2010) so need not be reviewed yet again here. What can be said is this:

- Participation in postsecondary education has increased dramatically almost everywhere so that some form of post-secondary credential is now roughly equivalent in value to what high school completion was a few decades ago.
- In most countries, the prestige (if not necessarily the quality) of postsecondary institutions is highly variable, which sets up a great deal of competition to get into the most prestigious or selective colleges and universities. Whether this competition is mediated through national examinations, high school grades, or through external tests such as the SAT, it still exercises powerful effects on what happens in high schools.
- The demand for skills in the labor market has increased but also changed in nature. It is not just that more skill is required but that different skills are needed. Intellectual skills are in higher demand. Work that used to be based on physical experience—for example, fixing machinery—now requires high levels of cognitive skill, such as reading manuals and computer outputs. Whether demand for skills has increased more rapidly than the supply of skilled people is a matter of dispute. There certainly continue to be, in all modern economics, considerable numbers of jobs that are badly paid and require relatively low skill levels; many economies, despite the rhetoric of high skills, report significant underemployment of educated young people (Livingstone, 2003).

In the face of these changes, high schools continue to be dominated by traditional academic courses and knowledge connected, whether appropriately or not, to preparation for postsecondary education (Lamb, 2011). Yet schools also recognize that a large number of students either do not plan to go immediately to postsecondary education or, in the school's view, do not have the capacity to be successful in that domain.

The dilemma is expressed by U.S. dropout research expert, Russ Rumberger:

> We have come to define high school success, as codified in graduation requirements, more and more narrowly by academic preparation for college. This is a disservice not just for our students but for our economy. Students will be more successful over their entire lives—as future students, workers, and citizens—if they achieve mastery in something during high school, whether it be academics, engine mechanics, or culinary arts. (Personal communication, May 2011)

Even more, much of what high schools provide is not particularly relevant even to those who do go on to postsecondary schools. One of the best examples is mathematics. Advanced math courses are required for students going to college and by many colleges for admission, even though only a tiny number of students actually study subjects in college requiring that level of mathematics and an even smaller proportion use advanced mathematics in their lives beyond schooling. Yet the mathematics that the overwhelming majority of people use every day, such as compound interest, an understanding of probability, and percentages, tends to be neglected in school curricula or is seen as "lower level" for less capable students. In other words, schools value—and are pushed by outside forces to value—a traditional academic curriculum even when this knowledge is not what would best serve students.

The tension between its academic preparation mission and the recognition that many students do not respond well to that mission has led to the creation of other program streams. Thus, vocational schools and programs were developed along with business or commercial programs or other programs that were intended to develop employment skills. Almost all secondary school systems around the world have some such differentiation, though the kinds of tracks, the proportions of students in them, the age at which differentiation starts, and students' ability to move from one track or program to another vary greatly across countries and systems.

While having different programs for different student needs and destinations seems desirable in theory, the problem is that so much evidence connects tracking with poorer overall outcomes for students. In the Programme for International Student Assessment (PISA) studies, countries with more streamed systems tend to have significantly poorer overall results (Organisation for Economic Co-operation and Development, 2010b). In North America, many studies show that students in nonacademic tracks have lower achievement, even controlling for initial ability, and that tracks increase social inequality among students (Gamoran, 2009; Oakes, 2005).

Although often justified in terms of a response to students' diverse skills, motivations, and plans, tracking is perhaps more a solution to the organizational challenges facing schools. It is simply much easier for schools as institutions to sort students into categories and then create programs for those different categories. Thus, one of the central problems with diverse program pathways is the question of whether placement decisions rest with students or with schools. In most systems, schools make considerable efforts to place students in programs that the schools feel are the best fit for them, even when students or parents disagree. This debate almost always involves parents resisting the school's wish to move a student out of a more academic program. These disputes are even more problematic given the evidence discussed earlier on our inability to predict student outcomes and the consistent overrepresentation of particular minority groups in lower track programs.

The truth is that despite the rhetoric that program streams are about meeting diverse student needs, high school programs are seen by just about everyone as hierarchical in terms of quality. Students themselves overwhelmingly see their assignment to different levels of courses as related to their capacity rather than to the relevance of these programs to each student's future. Staff members sometimes refer students to other programs largely because of the perception that the academic tracks are too difficult; however, "separate but equal" does not work any better in schools than it does in other settings, especially when the assignment of teachers to classes may further disadvantage students in lower status programs (a point discussed further a little later).

Some years ago, I visited several groups of students in Manitoba who were taking the 12th-grade examination in what was called "consumer mathematics"—a course designed to give lessons in practical mathematics such as mortgages, credit, or budgeting to students who were not taking more academic mathematics courses. When I asked these students why they were taking consumer math, not a single one said that is was more relevant to their lives and interests, even though this was the rationale for the course. They all gave the same response—that the other math courses were "too hard."

Many efforts have been made over the last 50 years to overcome the problems of tracking in high schools, but few of these efforts have had lasting success. The beliefs that traditional academic knowledge is the real curriculum, that some students are not capable of learning those skills, and that it is unreasonable and unfair to expect all students to achieve high levels of skill are all deeply embedded not only in the way high schools operate but also in the thinking of parents, students, and teachers and are a huge barrier to improving student outcomes. Even the best-intentioned teachers often struggle with the appropriate instructional techniques to teach diverse groups of students.

THE ROLE OF THE GED

Providing alternative qualifications can be an important part of an overall policy response to low levels of achievement. However, great care must be taken that the qualification carries real currency. Evidence shows that in many places, the GED does not provide access to postsecondary education or has only limited value in the job market (Lamb, 2011; Ou, 2008), in which case, it is really not of much value to students and should not be promoted. Some schools appear to use the GED as a way of pushing students out while still maintaining that the students are being served educationally. That does not seem a justifiable stance; schools should focus on students achieving learning, skills, and credentials that have broad acceptance and true value in the world beyond the schools. The focus should be on having as many students as possible earn a regular high school diploma.

VOCATIONAL EDUCATION

One of the main vehicles for program differentiation in high schools has been through vocational or technical programs that were intended to prepare students for specific jobs.

Vocational education presents a particular challenge. On the one hand, it is clearly much more related to the interests of many students than is the traditional academic program. There is some international evidence that participation in vocational programs is associated with better outcomes for those students (Lamb, Markussen, Teese, Sandberg, & Polesl, 2011). The problem is that participation in vocational education is also consistently higher among poor and minority students; as a result, it may cut them off from an important set of social and occupational opportunities that are connected to postsecondary education. Vocational education is often seen by schools as a place to put students who have less ability, less motivation, or both.

Some European countries, such as Germany or Finland, have been able to combine secondary education successfully with vocational and technical training. However, their success in doing so is primarily due to highly developed relationships between schools, employers, and labor unions such that participation in these programs is directly linked to qualifications for and employment in jobs that are satisfying and have good earnings. Strong apprenticeship systems closely linked to ongoing employment are typical in such systems. An OECD study (2010a) points out that these vocational models work well only in systems where schools are closely connected to the labor market. Even in these cases, participation in vocational education is typically highly related to student's socioeconomic status. Where these links to the labor market are not well developed, as in most of the English-speaking world, vocational education in secondary schools has a rather unsatisfactory track record (Grubb, 2011).

Since the nature of the labor market in Canada or the United States or Australia is not likely to change in that direction—and is not something that schools can control or even influence much in any case—those models are not likely to work well. Instead, other program models that combine high school with work education have been attempted, such as career academies. In these models, students typically choose some area of labor force activity and use a combination of courses and work experience to gain some depth of knowledge about it. The Pathways to Prosperity report from Harvard Graduate School of Education (2010) contains a number of examples of programs aimed at better connections to work, from career academies to "Project Lead the Way" to "High Schools That Work" to the Irvine Foundation's "Linked Learning District Initiative" in California. The Ontario specialist high skills major described later is another example. The goal of these programs is to keep the level of intellectual demand high and so to attract a broader range of students rather than seeing these as programs for students who are failing or disaffected. As Richard Teese (2011) put it, "The solution to equity lies in raising demands on young people, not lowering them through less challenging streams, including vocational options" (p. 355).

Given these complexities, how should high schools address the challenge of program differentiation? I suggest these seven principles to use in shaping and organizing high school programs:

- *High expectations.* We know that student performance tends to live up or down to the expectations of the school, so all programs have to embody high expectations. If students feel that their courses are considered "easy," it is much more difficult for teachers to create those high expectations.
- *Open futures.* One thing we know is that many students' lives will lead them in unanticipated directions. For all kinds of reasons, people rarely end up doing the things they planned when they were 16 years old. This means that school programs must build in flexibility and support students' later changes of plans.
- *Real credentials.* Whatever pathway students pursue should lead to credentials or qualifications that have real value either for further education, employment, or both. There is no room for programs that do not have a clear map to a desirable future.
- *Recovery.* Linked to both the former points, efforts should be made so that poor decisions or actions can be remedied and that more ambitious pathways can be pursued. Some teenagers will make impulsive and wrong choices; these cannot always be prevented, but a good system helps people recover from bad choices.
- *Self-direction.* Education should prepare students to take responsibility for their own lives, which implies giving them

real, meaningful, and increasing choices and responsibility during their high school years.

- *Whole school programming.* The co-curricular program is also an important element in the overall school program.
- *Partnerships.* Schools cannot provide all the desirable experiences from which students might benefit and so should look for opportunities to share programming with other agencies and organizations.

The following principles also suggest some direction for the organization of curriculum and programs in schools.

First, schools should err on the side of a more challenging curriculum. In particular, schools should minimize, if not eliminate, programs that do not lead to worthwhile outcomes in the form of entry to postsecondary education or other forms of training or to credentials that carry real recognition in the workplace for satisfying jobs. The question to ask is whether a course is connected to a good outcome for students (meaning more than just getting a credit). If it is not, then one must ask why the course is being offered.

Note that "more challenging" does not only mean "preparation for university." Challenging content can include anything that stretches students' minds and skills, that pushes them to learn more deeply, and that builds their sense of curiosity and engagement even if that is in an area that is not part of normal university entrance requirements. This point implies that the quality of teaching and learning is key no matter what program students are in, a point developed further in the next chapter.

Much programmatic effort should go toward trying to connect or reconnect with students who are off track for success and graduation. This means considering carefully the place of various levels of courses, alternative programs, credit recovery models, and other programs, several of which are discussed later in this chapter.

Finally, credentials matter. If all the qualifications offered by a school have some currency, either for postsecondary education or in the labor market (or, ideally, both), students are more likely to invest effort in attaining them. Credentials that do not lead to anything important will not be motivating or meaningful to students.

HOW MANY COURSES AND
HOW MUCH VARIETY?

For many years, high schools have regarded offering a large number of courses as an important way to meet student needs. These offerings vary on two, and occasionally three, dimensions. First, schools may add additional subjects ranging from the social sciences to the arts to various areas of career or vocational study.

Second, schools can differentiate within subjects either on the basis of content or level of challenge or both. Mathematics is typically differentiated for students who are considered to have less ability by offering courses that are more "applied" instead of what is considered more advanced material, such as calculus. The same may be done in other subjects. Alternatively, schools may simply add specialized courses—for example, different areas of history or science. These options may or may not be linked to the school's perception of students' skills.

Third, schools can differentiate courses based on delivery mode by offering courses via independent learning, online learning, or in partnership with postsecondary institutions (discussed in the next chapter).

Programs such as the International Baccalaureate or Advanced Placement are a hybrid in that they both offer different content and demand a particular level of ability.

The result of all this is that even a moderate sized high school may have hundreds of courses on the books. While scads of courses are often regarded with pride by schools, there is not much evidence that multiplying courses is an effective way to improve student outcomes. Indeed, the literature on school size suggests that smaller schools, which inevitably have fewer course options, do as well as or better than large schools with similar demographics (Leithwood & Jantzi, 2009).

The theory behind this book explains why that is so. Course content is not the main thing shaping student success; compared with relationships with adults and effective teaching, it is a relatively minor factor. Any subject matter can be interesting to students if well taught and any subject matter can be disengaging if badly taught; that lesson is abundantly clear from anyone's university experience in which quality of teaching entirely trumps subject matter. My own children went to a very small high school with very few course options and found that good teaching and a good school climate were the keys to feeling happy about their experience.

The argument in these pages, then, is that schools should not focus on adding or diversifying course offerings. Indeed, doing so can be counterproductive if it results in more segregation of students by ability (see the earlier discussions on tracking), if it limits the access of high-need students to excellent teaching, or if it excessively complicates organizing class schedules. Moreover, a multiplicity of classes tends to mean that some courses operate with smaller-than-optimal classes, which wastes resources that could be better used to support student success. The fundamental point is that focusing on the student experience is much more important than the specific courses.

I would make the same argument about Advanced Placement and International Baccalaureate programs. Sometimes schools use these programs as vehicles to recruit certain kinds of students. In other cases, they are a way to raise the aspiration level in a school. But whatever the motivation, these programs are not desirable if they result in more segregation of students or if they remove key staff from contact with students who need their skills. Systems should also consider carefully the incremental costs of these programs and whether the same resources could be employed more productively using other strategies.

ORGANIZING TEACHING

Improving school programming is not just a matter of which courses or programs are offered. It is also a matter of who teaches what and when. Timetables and teacher assignments are overlooked features of improving high schools, even though these are the central mechanisms through which students are assigned to programs and teachers. Although school timetables are such an important vehicle for organizing the school, they are the subject of relatively little research and of minimal training and support for the principals and vice principals who construct them. Consider the following issues:

- Timetables and the length of instructional periods are one factor in organizing school programming. Many schools spend considerable effort on changing their timetables but with little result. Any timetable system is likely to suit some teachers, students, and courses and not others, so at a system level, any change in timetable systems is unlikely to be worth the effort. In most schools, all instructional periods have the same length. Yet this seems unnecessary; if the weekly schedule had some longer and some shorter periods, it would be easier for teachers to adjust to particular subjects or groups of students.
- How should classes be organized? In most high schools, each class is organized in similar ways; students spend roughly equal time in groups of roughly equal size. Yet there is no reason other than convenience that this has to be so. It would be quite possible to organize a timetable that had classes of varying lengths on different days, as many colleges do. For example, one school instituted a different timetable with longer periods on Wednesdays as a way to accommodate field trips, labs, or other work that required extended periods of time.
- When should particular classes be scheduled? There are two elements to this issue–scheduling across terms and scheduling during the day. In the case of the former, providing a balance for students between different kinds of courses seems advisable so that the schedule has both more and less abstract learning tasks as part of most, if not all, days—just as elementary teachers slot music or physical activity into the day as a change from the more routine academic work. Many schools in Ontario found that their freshmen were more successful if the school did not schedule all their required academic courses in their first semester but spread them over the full year.

If there is evidence that students are more attentive and alert at some times during the school day than others, it makes sense to schedule the most demanding courses at times of maximum attendance and focus. Recent news reports have suggested that adolescent sleep needs should cause schools to start and end later. However, the research evidence on this issue is still scanty and quite insufficient to justify changing whole schools. Fortunately, that is not required; rather than making a big change based on weak evidence, one could experiment by adjusting the timing of particular courses to see what the effects were, especially if there were discussions with students about their preferences.

Timetables are also related to students' sense of coherence and continuity in the school day, which will be discussed in the next chapter. The fewer abrupt transitions students have, the less confusing their days are likely to be.

ASSIGNING STAFF

Another program issue of critical importance is which teachers are assigned to which students and classes. In many high schools, the most senior teachers are assigned to college-level courses for high school seniors or to Advanced Placement or International Baccalaureate classes. Equally, new teachers may be given the most challenging classes or the most different courses to teach, which militates against their success. While all this is understandable from the point of view of teacher satisfaction and seniority, both of which are important, it is not sensible from the standpoint of student needs. The goal must be to ensure that the most experienced and effective staff members spend a considerable part of their time with the students who most need their skills. It is surprising how few schools and school systems give any explicit attention to this goal. Of course, staff assignments must be balanced and teachers' desires about what classes they want to teach should be given serious consideration, since teacher morale is also a critical factor in school success. However, a collective discussion by staff of how best to organize teaching can often produce consensus on a better distribution of talent and skills than happens through the common process of simply accommodating the most senior teachers.

Teacher assignment is not the whole issue here, though. Much depends on the extent to which teaching in the school is a collective enterprise in which teachers are supporting each other. Susan Moore Johnson's work (2004) found that the degree of collegiality in a school was an important predictor of the success, satisfaction, and persistence in the profession of new teachers. No matter which teachers are assigned to the most challenging students and courses, their work can be eased by a strong network of mutual support among other staff.

HELPING TO REDUCE FAILURE RATES

What can schools do to reduce failure rates? Much of what is required will be discussed in Chapter 5 in regard to teaching, learning, and assessment practices. Another important element is the early warning system discussed in the previous chapter. However, there are some programmatic elements as well, which include schoolwide opportunities to recover or complete credits, opportunities for alternative programs, and specialized adaptations for particular groups of students.

Credit Rescue and Credit Recovery

Both these labels refer to organized structures that allow students to make up the work necessary for them to earn course credits. *Credit rescue* usually refers to situations in which the student is struggling while the course is still ongoing, whereas *credit recovery* refers to courses for which the student has already received a failing grade. In both situations, schools need to assign staff and time to support students so they can complete the work and gain the knowledge necessary to receive the credit. Given the strong relationship between failing a course and failing to graduate, efforts to keep students on track to graduation are vital in every school.

There are many different ways this work can be organized. The basic idea is this: teachers are assigned to work with small groups of students who are pursuing credit completion programs in a range of subjects; the teachers provide academic support, liaise with the original teachers to ensure that their requirements are met, and provide personal support to students. Sometimes these programs are built into the timetable, while in other places they are left informal.

These programs cannot be the main way in which schools address problems of failure. The real goal is to prevent students from getting into situations in which they are failing. Critics of credit rescue and credit recovery make the argument that these programs can result in students doing the minimum work required to pass a course; as students do less work, they devalue the courses and credits. That concern has to be taken seriously—although, of course, it also applies to every other course in a school. The point of any program is not simply for students to receive the credits any more than the point of high school is just to get a diploma. Everything a school does should be focused on helping students gain real success by developing meaningful knowledge and skills. Credit recovery is not about celebrating a 51% instead of a 46% in a course. It is about working with students to advance their learning and then recognizing that learning with the legitimate award of credits in consultation with the teachers who originally taught those courses to those students. The standards for credit recovery should be no less taxing than are the standards for any other course credit. At the same time, there is no reason to think that retaking an entire course is a better way for students to meet academic standards, and it is clearly a much less efficient way to do so.

Using Existing Program Models

A vast number of programs have been designed, recommended, or put in place over the years in effort to improve high school graduation rates. A report of the National Dropout Prevention Center (Hammond, Linton, Smink, & Drew, 2007) lists 50 such programs that have at least some evidence of impact. The long lists of factors associated with dropping out have led to an even longer list of programs designed to remedy those factors. If the problem is low starting achievement, then provide strong catch-up programs. If the problem is lack of parental support, help parents understand how to do this work better. If the problem is migrancy, provide shelter; if it is substance abuse, strengthen prevention programs, and so on.

These are important issues and many of the programs aiming to address them have noble goals and good ideas. However, the central argument of this book is that using a program model is too narrow; real success requires attention to a whole range of different issues in a way that takes into account the specificities of each school and district. Moreover, many packaged programs require schools to adopt them in total and in very specific ways and sometimes to pay quite high fees for materials and training. Some program providers inevitably become more concerned with their own revenues and survival, so they may not be as stringent as they should in determining whether they have the right solution to the needs of a given school or district. Packaged programs can have a place but should be used cautiously.

To be sure, there is much to be learned from the experience of others. All efforts to improve student outcomes should, as is the case in this book, be well grounded in the research evidence. Some off-the-shelf programs can offer good approaches on some issues and there may be cases where such a model offers a quick way to make some progress. But in the end, each school has to take ownership of its own strategy and that strategy has to be comprehensive and tailored. The danger of packaged programs is that they may reduce the school's thoughtfulness about its own students and their needs. A further danger is that too many such programs can lead to a school that has a whole range of programs but no overall approach and no integration or coherence among these programs.

CO-CURRICULUM

It has long been known that co-curricular activities such as sports or the arts (music, drama, etc.) have a strong effect in building relationships between some students and the school. There are several reasons for this, but the most important is that these activities provide an opportunity for success for students who may not have that opportunity in the academic program. They help build students' self-confidence in ways that carry over to the rest of the students' work. They also provide the school, including staff and other students, with a different view of those students by emphasizing their abilities instead of their limitations. However, few schools or systems systematically exploit that potential as part of a student success strategy. In general, students who participate in co-curricular programs are more likely to be students who are already invested in their schooling.

How might schools take more advantage of the co-curriculum as a success strategy?

- Actively recruit students into co-curricular programs. A school that is keeping a close eye on students who are struggling will also be able to see where co-curricular activities may represent an opportunity. Nor is this only a matter of students who already have athletic or artistic skills: many co-curricular activities also allow places for beginners—for example, to mount a drama production requires house managers, ticket managers, stage hands, and other roles that do not require a set of starting skills, just as sports teams need managers and trainers. As an instance, basketball was a very important part of my life for many years even though I was primarily a manager, since I had little talent as a player.

- Adjust or expand the range of co-curricular activities to meet students' interests. For example, students from some minority groups may value particular forms of art or music that the school has not previously offered but could offer now. Hip-hop music would be just one example. In parts of Canada, Aboriginal art has been a strong attraction and a route to success for some students. For others, the opportunity to be involved in drama productions, broadcasting, or DJ-ing has been important. Many more students are interested in sports than are able to play on school teams—unless the school finds ways to include more of them.

- Celebrate students' co-curricular achievements as a way of showcasing their skills and changing the way they are seen by others, which can then carry over into other parts of their schooling.

- Use the co-curriculum as a vehicle for encouraging academic performance, not as a threat. Many schools threaten to withdraw students from co-curricular activities if their academic performance slips. However, that would simply push students more toward leaving school altogether. Instead, schools should learn from the way that successful colleges work with athletes whose academic performance is weak—by providing support and encouragement instead of punishment. For example, schools can connect extracurricular activities to additional tutoring or counseling for students so that students have a supervised opportunity to get help and complete their school work as part of their other activities.

The co-curriculum is also an important vehicle for reaching into the community, as discussed more fully later, especially for people with skills and interests that are not present in the school staff.

ALTERNATIVE PROGRAMS AND SCHOOLS

There is definitely a place for alternative programs and schools in a secondary system. There are some students who are too estranged from the standard model of high school to be able to succeed, even with extensive support and real belief on the part of the school. Alternative programs or schools can take a wide variety of forms, but they usually involve a small number of staff working closely with a small number of students. These may be students with nonmainstream orientations or habits, students who are subject to bullying, or students who cannot cope with the multiple adults (and other students) that are inevitably part of a regular high school. They may also be students, such as those mentioned in Chapter 1, who left school earlier and now want to return but do not feel able to face their former institution.

Decisions about whether to offer alternative programs and which ones should depend on a deep knowledge of students and a careful assessment of whether these are the best ways to assist them in graduating.

The challenge is to ensure that alternative programs do not become dumping grounds for students that the main school does not want and that these programs' existence does not become an excuse for other staff or programs to ignore students' real needs and interests. The tendency to look for alternative placements for students seen as "difficult" is deeply ingrained in large institutions like schools and must be guarded against at all times. It is worrying that according to Educational Testing Service (ETS) data (Barton, 2005), the existence of alternative schools or programs is increasing steadily in the U.S. and is most common where minority enrollment is highest though there is little or no evidence on the success of these programs. A study of alternative schools in California (McLaughlin, Atukpawu, & Williamson, 2008) showed that these schools varied greatly in purpose and quality but were often seen by the system as "dumping grounds" for difficult students.

Any school or district offering alternative programs—and most should be offering some—needs to monitor carefully which students are in these programs and how successful the programs are. Participating in an alternative program should almost always be the student's choice, not a requirement imposed on them by the school.

School districts have experimented with a range of alternative programs intended to meet the needs of groups who were not doing well in mainstream schools. Thus Toronto has Triangle, a school primarily for lesbian, gay, bisexual, and transgender (LGBT) students. Several western Canadian cities have Aboriginal schools that aim to provide a more comfortable place for Canadian Indian or Métis students who are estranged from regular schools. Toronto also recently opened (though at the elementary level) an Afrocentric school, in recognition of the gaps in achievement for African Canadian students.

While each of these schools has made an important contribution, one of the most important things to note about them is that the vast majority of students in each of these minority groups, whether LGBT, Aboriginal, or African American, will not be attending alternative schools but will be in mainstream high schools. Mainstream schools must continue to work on being more welcoming to and more successful with these students and their families. The alternative schools or programs can provide models, but they cannot themselves carry the weight of equity for all students.

Program Needs of Specific Groups

Alternative programs are one approach to learning for students for whom mainstream programs do not work well. However, there are other options that do not require the same kind of separation and still provide alternative formats or options for particular students who may be struggling.

One group that requires attention is students who are returning after the normal graduation year to try to complete their graduation requirements or students who are returning to school after one or more years away. Many such students do end up in adult education or alternative programs, but sometimes they arrive there by default. There are many other ways schools could accommodate such students programmatically:

- Build an individual education plan for each such student, monitored regularly by a teacher whom the student likes and respects so that the problems of the previous year do not immediately recur.
- Create support groups of returning students who can share challenges and strategies.
- Provide specific instruction in learning strategies, such as study habits or writing skills, where these are seen as significant problems.
- Enable part-time study.
- Provide tutoring programs for returning students as additional support for staying on track.
- Create classes for returning students in a few key subjects where failure rates tend to be highest.
- Make sure that teachers are aware of these students, offer their support, and can be flexible on issues such as attendance or assignment due dates when required.
- Move students to another school where they may have a fresh start and less constraint from their past behavior and relationships.

These provisions can often be accommodated without creating a separate program, provided that the school pays attention to their students' needs.

Another group with particular programming needs is students, mainly young women, who are also parenting. In addition to the obvious (though often hard to meet) need for good child care and reasonable housing, these students may also benefit from some of the previously listed proposals such as reduced course loads, altered timetables, and flexibility in doing their work to reflect the requirements of caring for young children. Most of all, they need sympathetic and supportive teachers who, while recognizing their situation, are still committed to their learning.

For some students, any or all of these adaptations might increase their motivation and chances of graduating. The point of all this is not to create a panoply of separate programs for separate groups, which can have negative effects on the coherence of the school as a whole. The main focus is for the school to begin with student needs and situations rather than starting with the current program organization and pushing students to fit it whether that is what they need or not.

CONCLUSION

Creating an appropriate program structure in high schools is a challenging task. It requires the usual attention to students' interests, staff capacity, college entry requirements, and labor market issues, but it takes something more than that. Central to the whole effort is the idea that the school program must be designed to encourage the highest possible level of performance by the greatest number of students and so must pay attention to student diversity in ways that extend far beyond offering a few electives or different difficulty levels of the same subject. The key must be programs that increase the likelihood of "a good outcome for every student." This chapter has suggested various possibilities for moving in that direction. The next chapter addresses teaching and learning more specifically.

Take-Aways

- A central challenge for high schools is how to balance students' diverse interests and skills while also offering all students opportunities for postsecondary education and meaningful employment.

- In general, tracks and streams in high schools lead to programs of unequal value with poor and minority students disproportionately placed in programs that have less value and produce poorer outcomes. Schools should generally try to provide a challenging curriculum for as many students as possible.

- Various forms of vocational education can be valuable only if they are closely linked to real labor market credentials and opportunities.

- More variety in courses is not necessarily related to better outcomes for students; good teaching is more important than a wider choice of courses.

- Organizational factors, such as which courses are scheduled when and who teaches which students, are important but do not get enough attention in many systems.

- The co-curriculum is an important vehicle for many students and should be used accordingly.

- Strong efforts to keep students from failing courses are vital and much more effective than dealing with failure after the fact.

- Various alternative programs can be useful only if they do not become dumping grounds for unsuccessful students.

CHAPTER FIVE

Improving Teaching and Learning

A ll the changes we might make in adult-student relationships or in school programs will not be sufficient
unless there are also changes in the daily learning experiences of
students. The heart of schooling lies in the work that students and
their teachers do every day, yet this is in many ways the hardest
thing to change in high schools for reasons outlined in Chapter 1.
Notable among these are the effects of subject specialization on
students and teachers, the pressures exerted by the expectations
of postsecondary institutions, and the need schools have to sort
students into categories related to their presumed futures. All
these factors make it hard to change teaching and learning practices, which is one reason that so many high school reforms focus
on structural features, such as school size, teacher-advisor systems, or graduation requirements.

However, the reality to keep in mind is this:

*Improving daily teaching and learning is essential to achieving
better high school outcomes; to do this requires a thoughtful and
specific strategy.*

To say that changing teaching and learning is difficult does
not mean that we should stop trying to enact changes. Many
things are difficult but can still be done; this is one of them. There

are some key tools that can be used to improve teaching and learning practices—tools that do *not* emphasize teacher evaluation or merit pay, both of which I believe to be ineffective strategies.

Let's start with the overall purpose of instructional change.

The central goal of teaching and learning in all schools should be to engage students in tasks that have a high level of challenge and will therefore stretch their skills and knowledge. Education is about helping people to use their brains. (I will return later to the issue of hands-on education.) Much evidence from psychology tells us that people thrive on challenge when it stretches them while staying within their potential. Solving puzzles or overcoming barriers of any kind is enormously satisfying to people, as is becoming good at something one values. People are least interested in routine, easy-to-do things, whether those are so-called basic skills at school or repetitive tasks at work. If a task is too difficult, people will try to avoid it, so the key is to find the right balance of challenge and possibility.

Schools should be trying to develop instruction composed of three main elements: the right level of intellectual challenge, a coherent experience within and across courses, and a high level of interest or relevance. Moreover, this effort is required for all students in all courses and is particularly important for students in lower tracks.

A good start to any program of instructional improvement is to try to see learning in the high school the way students see it. Any teacher or school leader who wants to understand the high school experience should spend a couple of days as a student. That experience would remind us of how far most students' experiences are from the ideals in the goal statements of most school systems. As reported earlier, many students spend much of their time in high school being bored or unengaged and they can be quite expressive in showing discontent by withdrawing their attention and support or even by being actively disruptive.

Many educators see students' low level of engagement as a fundamental challenge or obstacle to better teaching. But even though students do not necessarily show a high level of motivation in schools, virtually all students are highly motivated when engaged in something that they care about (see box on page 91). One of the serious disconnects in education policy is between our growing understanding of human motivation (e.g., Dweck, 2007)

Fires in the Mind

Kathleen Cushman's book (2010) is based on discussions with 160 young people about the things that really engaged and motivated them. She found that every one of these students, even those unsuccessful in school, had something in their lives that they cared about and in which they invested large amounts of time and energy, from car repairs to video games to sports to making clothes. Students wanted to be good at these things. They spent large amounts of time, did plenty of research, and gave lots of careful thought to their choices and activities.

Among Cushman's conclusions were the following:

- Adults and other young people played a large role in generating interest; students can find many things interesting under the right conditions. Students largely "gravitated to something because it looked like fun . . . and because someone gave them a chance and encouraged them."

- Adults, including teachers, were very important in helping them over the rough spots in their skill development and in supporting their efforts and giving them the practice they needed.

- Motivation is a combination of caring about something and believing one can learn to do it well. Both are important.

- Students had many suggestions for ways in which their teachers and schools could support and encourage them.

and the way we think about education policy and organize our schools. Young people want and can achieve the internal space that Csíkszentmihályi called *flow* (Csíkszentmihályi, 1990), where time and space fall away due to full engagement in the task. It is very important for schools to consider how to create the conditions in which more students do care about what they do at school and how more students can be in the flow space.

These ideas about challenge and meaning are not new, yet much evidence shows that low-demand tasks, such as recalling facts, continue to be common and even dominant practice in most high school classrooms (National Research Council, 2003).

Here is a recent description by Harvard professor Richard Elmore, based on extensive observations in many schools across the United States:

I spend a lot of time in classrooms . . . a lot of it in high schools . . . Mostly what I see in my visits to middle- and upper-grade classrooms are examples of . . . "the bargain"—"you give me order and attendance, I'll give you passing grades and [minimal] homework." The only other public institution in our society that works this way, with this degree of focus and dedication, is the prison system . . . For most students, the pace of work is like a thick sludge, moving in no particular direction toward a destination defined by escape. U.S. secondary schools, it seems, are primarily custodial institutions, designed to hold adolescents out of the labor force and to socialize them to adult control . . . I wonder . . . [whether people] are aware of what classrooms in American secondary schools actually look like—the dismal, glacial, adult-centered, congenially authoritarian, mindless soup in which our children spend the bulk of their days. (Elmore, 2011)

While Elmore's characterization may be particularly negative, it is clear that teaching practices have not changed much, even after many years of recognizing that higher-order tasks are required for truly meaningful and effective education. For 40 years, we have been hearing that instruction in high schools is too teacher centered, too focused on talk, and too much about the learning of facts. I can remember hearing decades ago the old adage that copying notes from the board (and later from the overhead projector, then from the whiteboard or the Internet) is the fastest way to get information from the teacher's book to the students' book without it passing through anyone's brain. In preparing this book, I ran across some correspondence and media reports from 40 years ago on the efforts of the principal of a high school in Campbell River, British Columbia, to create a school with more interesting instruction and more engaged students, which was strongly supported by his teachers and students but was eventually scuttled as being simply too different. In another instance, a superintendent in Winnipeg told me that a committee in his district had agreed that they should develop an alternative high school "as long as it looked pretty much like our other existing high schools." Despite all the advocacy over the years, not much seems to have changed. Indeed, high schools today may be more traditional than they were 40 years ago.

Another challenge in improving high school instruction is that in most high schools, the focus is on the curriculum as expressed in individual courses with little attention to schoolwide approaches. Teachers, naturally enough, think about the courses they are teaching and students think about what they have to do to pass those courses. It is assumed that somehow all of these separate pieces will somehow make a whole, even though in most high schools, nobody is thinking about or responsible for achieving such coherence. In practice, students' experience ends up being very fragmented in terms of tasks, knowledge, and procedures, with high variation in what students are asked to do and how they are asked to behave across a school. Every 40 minutes or hour, they enter a place with a new set of expectations, rules, tasks, and roles. There is little carryover from one class to another. Knowledge and skills do not tend to build over a student's years in high school, with the possible exception of those few subjects where one year's learning feeds the next.

A third oft-cited concern about high schools has to do with the relevance of the learning. "Why do we have to know this?" is a question students regularly ask, whether it is about trigonometry, organic chemistry, or world history. I will say more on this point a little later, but my main contention is that complaints about relevance are often really complaints about teaching methods and that much of the problem of relevance vanishes when good teaching and learning practices are used.

These problems in high school instruction are well known. The fact that they continue to be identified after so many years strongly suggests that serious barriers to change exist. The stance of this book is that recommendations for improvement have to be realistic in order to have some chance of making a difference. Given how many reports and proposals there have been for improvement in high schools and how few of them seem to have caught on in a significant way, such realism has perhaps not been a strong point in past.

COMPREHENSIVE REFORM MODELS

Because the focus of this book is on change in all schools, I do not recommend particular school models such as Accelerated

Schools, Big Picture Schools, Essential Schools, or the various comprehensive school reform models of a decade or so ago. As noted in the previous chapter, it's not that there is anything wrong with these models. Many of them have very worthwhile features and share many of the ideas put forward in these pages. Rather, my concern is that the track record for adopting and sustaining innovation packages of this kind is not good.

In the 1980s and 1990s, the United States made significant efforts to introduce comprehensive school reform models, first through the New American Schools program and then through comprehensive school reform. Both initiatives involved very substantial efforts to put in place full-scale alternative approaches to schooling. Yet the evaluation of these programs showed that few of them made a significant or lasting difference (Rumberger, 2011). There could be many reasons for this. Some programs were too ambitious, required too much change, needed more skills and support than most schools or systems could muster, or were simply based on a wrong theory of action. In other cases, new programs were adopted but then dropped by a new leader a few years later. An equal concern is that people feel that implementing a program is the answer to improving schools, when in reality any program model will raise new questions and still require lots of thinking and problem solving. The basic approach in this book is that the requirement for successful improvement is less a well-defined model than a clear set of goals followed by relentless and sustained effort to change practices and policies. That is the approach that seems to work best, as described in this Harvard report on successful schools:

> The main lesson from the presentations was that student achievement rose when leadership teams focused thoughtfully and relentlessly on improving the quality of instruction. Core groups of leaders took public responsibility for leading the charge to raise achievement. Stakeholders crafted mission statements that later helped keep them on track, planned carefully (sometimes with outside assistance) for how they would organize learning experiences for teachers, clearly defined criteria for high-quality teaching and student work, and implemented ways that engaged all faculty members. As they implemented their plans, these schools

carefully monitored both student and teacher work in order to continuously refine their approaches. (Harvard Graduate School of Education, 2010)

Various off-the-shelf program models can offer useful guidance on some of this work, but none of them avoid the obligation each school and system has to do this work in a sustained way.

To promote better instructional practice in high schools, I suggest a focus on four kinds of changes. First, high schools need to help teachers work collectively to improve their daily teaching practices by, for example, making more use of the strong connection many teachers feel to their subject associations. Second, strategies to promote greater student engagement in classrooms and in the school as a whole are also potentially very powerful. Third, effective student assessment practice is the best single lever to change student experiences and the most likely to be embraced by many teachers, if carefully implemented. Finally, schools could do much to encourage more independent learning by students in a variety of ways. Other strategies, such as effective use of data and information technology, are also useful in my view but not as powerful overall as these four. The point of all these changes is the same: to raise the level of challenge and interest for students so that they consider their education to be something that deserves their genuine effort.

But before turning to these issues, a few words are needed on the matter of "relevance" of the curriculum and the related idea that some students need to work with their hands rather than have solely intellectual challenges.

RELEVANCE

When I was involved in high school reform as a high school student and young school board member, much of the discussion was centered on a more relevant curriculum. Relevance continues to be an important issue in discussions today; it is one of the new 3 Rs—rigor, relevance, and relationships.

In this book, I take a different view of relevance. My own experience of learning and my observations of many other settings have convinced me that virtually any learning can be relevant—in the sense of fascinating—to learners if it is well presented and effectively taught. As an undergraduate university student, I ran orientation sessions for incoming freshman students. My advice was always to find out who the outstanding professors were and to take whatever courses they were teaching. Another expression for the same point was when my eldest daughter, who was not engaged in her high school courses, came home early in her first year of university classes to announce, "The Etruscans were so interesting!" In other words, good teaching creates relevance. One can observe the same phenomenon in virtually any high school; teachers are able to engage and interest students no matter what the subject. Cushman (2010) reports that being around an adult who was passionate about something was one of the main ways that young people found an interest of their own to pursue in depth.

This is not to dismiss issues of curriculum content, which were discussed in Chapter 4, but simply to say that it is possible to have a very broad definition of what counts as relevant to students; it is not just a matter of having courses on the things students think they care about. Of course, it makes sense to offer courses in areas where students have a strong interest or to adapt existing courses to the same end, but course content and syllabi are less important than what happens when teachers and students meet. Indeed, one of the most satisfying parts of education for both students and teachers is to see students become engaged intellectually in a whole new field or set of ideas. Sadly, too often students do not get this experience until postsecondary education—and some never have their eyes and minds opened in that wonderful way.

HANDS-ON LEARNING

This phrase is often used to suggest that some learners, usually those struggling with the traditional curriculum, need a different approach that is somehow less abstract and more grounded in real experience. Although intuitively appealing, on closer examination the implications of this idea are not at all clear.

First, all learning involves some cognitive component. There is no real learning in any subject without engaging the mind actively. The most concrete tasks, such as repairing a machine or cooking a meal, are at least as much cognitive as they are physical. All physical performance, whether sports or dance or making music or visual art, has a large cognitive element to it as well. All skilled trades now require good reading skills, and almost all require strong mathematic competencies in order to do the hands-on work. It is not sensible to talk about hands-on learning as something different from cognitive work; the two are inextricably connected.

Perhaps the idea of hands-on learning, then, is to have more practical activities, such as demonstrations. But learning that involves practical activities is powerful for all students. For all of us, doing or seeing something provides a stronger learning experience than does just reading about it or thinking about it. Increasing amounts of practical activity should be part of good instruction everywhere. Consider the popularity in schools of robotics competitions, which are both intellectually challenging and intensely practical. Nor is it evident what this practical component would mean in many areas of the curriculum. Is hands-on learning in mathematics about using manipulatives or solving real-world problems instead of those in the textbook? Does hands-on in science mean more experiments? Why wouldn't those be good practices for all students?

Finally, there is the worry that hands-on learning is code for giving students less challenging and interesting work, rather like replacing reading in elementary classrooms with coloring. But the right level of challenge is a central element in creating engaging classrooms and schools. Students need work that it not too easy for them—though also not too hard.

A reasonable conclusion is that hands-on learning alone is not a helpful way of thinking about what students need and should be subsumed instead under broader ideas of engaging learning, as discussed throughout this chapter.

COLLECTIVE WORK BY TEACHERS

The fastest and most powerful way to change anyone's behavior is by putting that person among other people who behave differently. People are very inclined to adapt their behavior to fit in with the group. Schools are no different. Although there is much talk about the isolation of the classroom, teachers are, in fact, deeply influenced by their colleagues and by the overall tone of a school. It is very difficult for any individual teacher to be too much out of step with the dominant approach in her or his school.

The Organisation for Economic Co-operation and Development's (OECD) Teaching and Learning International Survey (TALIS) (OECD, 2011) found that most teachers report that they do not work very often with colleagues. At the same time, we know that teachers have a strong preference for collective learning. Thus, a critical element for change in schools is providing carefully structured opportunities for teachers to work together to create the right kind of positive and energized climate and to improve their instructional practice in ways that evidence tells us are likely to improve student learning.

Knowledge and Teaching Practice

The practices discussed in this chapter are all based on substantial research evidence yet are not common in schools, which raises the wider issue of the role of research in teaching. Professions are characterized by the pursuit of good common practice rooted in evidence of effectiveness. Research plays a vital role in every profession, since it creates the grounding for good practice. But in a strong profession, the members own their collective practice. Research is not, as it often now is in education, something that happens elsewhere and then has its results thrust onto practitioners. It is instead something professionals own as the essence of their identity. There is, in the ideal profession, an ongoing dialogue between research and practice, in which each deeply informs the other and neither has a superior position. The findings of one are tested through the other in both directions, and the best results become the foundation of improved professional practice. It is this spirit that should animate teachers' collective work—a spirit of inquiry in which the best professional thought and knowledge is melded with the best independent research to guide increasingly well-grounded and effective practices, which are then embraced by the whole profession.

Learning Communities

Much has been written about the merits of professional learning communities, which have become a commonplace topic within schools. The idea of collective learning is now well entrenched in our thinking about education, though not necessarily in practice. It is important to keep in mind that having a professional learning community is not the goal; the point is to focus collective attention on effective shared practice. Learning communities, therefore, need to root their work in good evidence of effective practice, drawn both from the broader research literature and from careful examination of their own local data and experience. It's not enough to talk about issues; the task is to look at how people are doing their work and how it could be done better (Elmore, 2004; Harris & Jones, 2010). The potential power of this approach is shown in the many good books on collective learning by teachers with lots of examples of how this work can happen (e.g., City, Elmore, Fiarman, & Teitel, 2009; Du Four, Du Four, Eaker, & Many, 2006; Fullan, 2006), as well as in the quote below from the *New York Times*:

> After years of high dropout rates and dismal test scores, a group of teachers at the high school in Brockton [Massachusetts] organized a schoolwide campaign that involved reading and writing lessons in every class in all subjects, including gym . . . [In] this year and last, Brockton outperformed 90% of Massachusetts high schools . . . In engineering the turnaround, the self-appointed group determined that reading, writing, speaking, and reasoning were the most important skills and recruited nearly every educator in the building—not just English [teachers], but math [teachers], science [teachers], and guidance counselors—to teach those skills. The committee devised a rubric to help teachers understand what good writing looks like and devoted faculty meetings to instructing department heads on . . . [the use of good writing]. Then, the school's 300 teachers were trained in small groups. The committee offered help to reluctant teachers, and since all committee members were in the union, scrupulously hewed to union rules. (Dillon, 2010)

A rich research literature (best reviewed in Timperley, Wilson, Barrar, & Fung, 2007) discusses the conditions for effective professional learning in schools. This learning needs to focus on the real tasks of instruction above all else. It requires external input to challenge current ways of thinking. It has to be sustained over time and supported by school leaders. It has to be aligned with student assessment and teacher evaluation practices. But the division of secondary schools into subjects means that some strategies must also be adapted and that simply bringing together teachers from across a high school may not be effective.

One approach is to make more use in secondary schools of the subject areas because that is how most high school teachers identify themselves. Teachers in the same or similar subject areas can work together in or across schools to discover how they can be more effective in their work. Associations of subject teachers, whether in language or mathematics or science, can offer guidance to their members that will be accepted in ways that proposals from school administrators will not, because the former are seen by most teachers as knowledgeable peers whose ideas should carry weight. Most professional learning in schools can and should be organized through the professional subgroups to which teachers already feel allegiance.

The second strategy involves schoolwide or systemwide activities in important areas that look at common approaches or practices while still recognizing differences across subjects and departments. These common areas include assessment (discussed more fully below), higher-order skills, and literacy and numeracy across the curriculum. These are areas in which there can be great benefit from schoolwide discussion, as long as there is not an attempt to force all teachers into a common approach. In effective collective learning and discussion, increasingly common practices should naturally emerge. Administrators need to resist the temptation to try to force a consensus; instead, they should work to have greater commonality in practice emerge from teachers' collective work.

Consider literacy across the curriculum as an example: if this issue were presented as "all teachers must teach writing skills" as defined by the English department, it would run up against much resistance from other teachers. If, instead, the discussion is about how literacy skills manifest themselves in different subject areas and how the teaching of those subjects would benefit from some explicit attention to literacy skills, most teachers will engage in discussions about what that might mean for how they organize and teach their classes.

EFFECTIVE STUDENT ASSESSMENT

Student assessment practices provide one of the best levers for generating collective learning and changes in practice in high schools. This is because assessment—what counts for grades or is on the exam—deeply affects what teachers do, what students do, and what both parties care about. We also know that good assessment practices have strong positive effects on student learning.

The most important assessment practices can be summed up fairly readily by drawing on various sources, including the work of Dylan William (2008), John Hattie (2008), Doug Reeves (2010), Fred Newmann, Walter Secada, and Gary Wehlage (1995), and others. The rationales for these practices are relatively self-evident and will not be repeated here. The key aspects include the following elements:

- Clear criteria for and examples of good work, with student input into the formation of the criteria so that students understand clearly what quality work looks like
- More focus on the higher-order skills of analysis, synthesis, thinking about alternatives, and problem solving, especially in courses that tend to have lower expectations for students (Clear criteria and examples, by the way, tend to lead to more attention to higher-order skills.)
- More consistent assessment criteria across subjects and courses so that students can make wider use of generic learning and metacognitive skills
- Alternative ways to demonstrate learning that are consistent with the goals and criteria, such as different kinds of writing, alternatives to writing, or combinations of group and individual work
- Grading systems that are demonstrably valid, reliable, and fair, thus reducing subjectivity in the awarding of grades
- Multiple opportunities to demonstrate learning, with evaluation based on the most consistent evidence of overall learning, which also means an end to noneducational practices, such as averaging grades across a term or course
- Ongoing use of assessment data to inform teaching practice

If these elements were widespread in secondary class-rooms, they would inevitably lead to very significant changes in how teachers taught and what students did and learned. They would also yield increased student engagement and sat-isfaction. Students with lower achievement levels are likely to derive the greatest benefit from more interesting instruction and assessment.

The best way to increase consistency in assessment is through teachers working together to discuss and evaluate student work. In every setting where teachers are involved in moderating grad-ing of, say, large-scale tests, they report this as being some of the best professional development of their careers, with significant impact on how they teach and assess students. Douglas Reeves (2010) wrote about the power of bringing teachers together and allowing them to discover that they hold very different standards for student work, even in the same subjects and courses. Despite this compelling evidence, teachers' collective review of student work remains an unusual professional development activity in most school systems. This work is not hard to organize (it can be built into staff meetings or other existing professional develop-ment activities) and because teachers find it stimulating, it has high potential as a change activity.

The collective discussion of student work is also likely to lead to greater consistency in demands on students across years and courses and to increased coherence in the instructional program as a whole. As teachers become more aware of what other col-leagues are asking students to do, they can modify their own work to be complementary or supplementary across courses, subjects, and grades. The benefits for student learning are obvious.

Another element related to assessment has to do with timing. In most schools, students are asked to complete most of their work in the short period just before grades are issued. This inevitably means that students face a barrage of tests and assignments in a short period of time, making it very hard (if not impossible) for even the most organized of students to do their best work. Equally, for many students there are significant blocks of time where they are not being asked to produce much work at all. There is no reason that this has to be the case. A school that sets out to organize itself so that student work was spread reasonably over an entire term could largely eliminate this end-of-term crush, which benefits all those concerned, including teachers who are normally swamped with grading during the same short period. If good assessment practices are in place, linked with the recovery and rescue programs discussed in Chapter 4, there is no reason to push everything into the same two or three weeks of each term.

Improving assessment practices in a school can only happen through discussion among teachers within and across departments. It can be a tricky business since teachers are used to particular ways of organizing their teaching and assessment. But if teachers work together, they can find ways to meet their instructional needs and also find fairer ways to distribute students' work over each term, which benefits teachers as well as students. Input from students can play an important part in this activity by helping teachers organize tasks and timing in ways that work for all parties. This is an instance of a change that can clearly be win-win for all concerned.

Finally, in regard to assessment, high schools have to find ways of combining the traditional subjects with the new skills that students require, such as teamwork and independent learning. There are quite a few different sets of these so-called 21st-century skills floating around now, though the various lists tend to have much in common.

Schools have used various approaches to try to build skill coherence and meta-skills (skills such as how to learn) into their work. Creating new courses to focus on these skills defeats the point of integration and is very difficult to do for various logistical reasons. Most curricula now include these new skills among their goals, though typically they do not get very much attention in the work students are asked to do. But if assessment practices are linked to these skills, they will get more attention from schools and students. For example, in Ontario, the provincial test results for literacy and numeracy show that students are strongest on so-called basic skills and weakest on higher-order skills. Schools cannot improve their performance, then, by practicing test-taking skills or by drilling on the basics; they have to do the work of teaching deeper comprehension skills. In this way, good assessment practices support good teaching.

Other assessment practices that support this broader approach to skills can also be mentioned. For example, some schools use culminating assignments with public displays and evaluation (Cambridge, 2010; Harris Stefanakis, 2010). Various sources already cited show that public performances can be highly motivating for students. Other schools use portfolios put together over the student's entire high school experience to show a wider range of skills than simply meeting course requirements. Portfolios, which seem intuitively a desirable idea, have not caught on well in schools, probably because they do not fit well into the existing structure of courses. Still, the idea of having some multiyear activity in the school that focuses on wider learning beyond the content of specific courses has much potential as a way to bring greater integration to what could otherwise be a very fragmented experience.

Finally, reporting to parents (and students themselves) can and should also be based on principles of formative assessment. For example, student-led conferencing, common in elementary schools but not in high schools, involves students in the organization and presentation of their achievements to parents as part of the reporting process. Giving students a role in reporting is likely to increase their sense of responsibility for their work and results.

STUDENT ENGAGEMENT IN TEACHING AND LEARNING

In Chapter 3, the importance of student voice and engagement in schools was outlined but primarily at the level of the school as an institution. Yet student engagement is even more important in regard to daily teaching and learning.

This kind of input increases student commitment to the work because students not only have some say in what the work is, but they are also much more likely to understand what is being asked of them and to influence the work in ways that make their doing it more likely. Both those factors increase the likelihood of success in addition to the positive psychological impact of being asked for one's views.

Student feedback is key to teachers' understanding of how students are thinking about their work and therefore it is also key to teachers' ability to modify their lessons to be most effective.

Hattie's (2008) meta-analysis shows that good feedback from teachers to students and vice versa is a very powerful way to improve outcomes. One of my favorite stories in this regard is a teacher of fourth-grade health who asked her class to help her teach the course better. The students looked at the curriculum and reported back to her on which parts of it they already knew quite a bit about and which parts would need more intensive teaching from her. She was stunned by the difference this made in the way students engaged with the class, changing it from a chore assigned by her to something they cared about. Extensive empirical literature (e.g., Thiessen & Cook-Sather, 2007) supports the efficacy of such engagement.

What does this mean in practical terms in a school? There are many ways teachers can solicit input from students beyond those already mentioned:

- Have a discussion at the start of each course about the objectives, purpose, and content of the course, coupled with students' ideas on how this information could best be learned by them.
- Have students participate in creating scoring rubrics for various assignments.
- Have a discussion with students about the appropriate balance of lecture, independent work, group work, and homework.
- Give individual students more choices about course work—what they do, when they do it, and how they do it—perhaps from a range of alternatives or by giving students opportunities to suggest alternatives to assignments given by teachers.

Though some teachers fear that such approaches could lead to them losing control over the classroom or could require more work on their part, engaging students in these ways is more likely to result in increased student commitment, effort, and satisfaction and can also reduce discipline problems with issues such as late or incomplete assignments. Engagement is not about teachers ceding responsibility for what happens in their classrooms. It is about bringing students in as real partners.

Student Voice in the School and Classroom

The Manitoba School Improvement Program (MSIP) is an independent body that works with high schools in Manitoba, Canada, on school improvement programs. MSIP supports a whole range of student voice activities in these schools (Pekrul & Levin, 2007). These activities were all linked to improved school performance and student outcomes. They included adding students to school improvement teams, implementing regular surveys of student attitudes, and starting a student mentoring program for new or struggling students. A particularly interesting initiative involved students working on research projects that gathered data on outcomes of former students. Students did this work as part of one of their courses, thereby learning various research and data analysis skills and then presented their findings to school staff and parents. The students involved found the experience very powerful, not only in terms of learning new skills but also in gaining an understanding of how their high school experience would affect their later lives. Both staff and students were challenged by a situation in which students now had relevant knowledge that staff did not, the opposite of what happens most of the time.

Examples of student voice in secondary schools can be found at the following websites:

- Soundout: www.soundout.org
- California Association of Student Councils: http://www .casc.net/programs/sabe/
- Kentucky Department of Education, Refocusing Secondary Education Student Voice Summit: http://www.education .ky.gov/KDE/Instructional+Resources/High+School/ Refocusing+Secondary/What+Kentucky+Students+Say/

THE ROLE OF INFORMATION TECHNOLOGY

One of the huge debates in education today, and one closely related to student engagement, is the appropriate role of information technology. That debate is not new; for the last 50 years, since the introduction of television, pundits have been talking about how technology would fundamentally change schooling and how schools would have to transform or become irrelevant.

That claim was made for television, VCRs, and computers, and is now made for laptops, whiteboards, and PDAs.

There does not, however, seem to be much evidence that the claim is true. Studies of the impact of new technologies on student outcomes have been consistently disappointing for 30 years, showing little difference whether traditional methods or new technologies are used (for one instance, see Cuban, 2001). Schools hardly seem to have been revolutionized in any way by these technologies. Indeed, it might be argued that the constant effort to equip schools with technology has been a rather substantial waste of time and money compared to other efforts that might have been made to improve teaching and learning. Consider recent efforts to give all students laptops—many of these efforts were suspended after a couple of years because they were too costly and did not show much result (Tamim, Bernard, Borokhovski, Abrami, & Schmid, 2011).

Technology advocates have responded for at least 20 years now that the problem is inadequate teacher training. But it seems unlikely that teachers will ever catch up to students in a world in which technology is changing so rapidly. In fact, a teacher who was completely up-to-date with the technology use of 2005—not that long ago—would be entirely behind the times now, and the same is likely to be true every few years. Given that many people teach for decades and that turnover of the teaching force happens slowly, it seems unlikely that either school equipment or teacher skills can be kept current in the rapidly changing technological world.

This position does not mean that technology is unimportant or can be ignored. The current trend does seem somewhat different in that the new wave of technology is closely tied to the way students learn and experience the world. It is also changing the way people of all ages learn. Schools do have to come to terms with these developments in some way. School practices that ban cell phones, for example, are doomed to be ineffective because phones are so much a central part of the way students now live. These policies also seem counterproductive in that they treat students as immature and in need of control rather than as active participants in their own education.

A better strategy for technology would be to engage students in discussion of how the school should respond to these issues. Technology is the one area in schools where it is widely accepted that students will know more than teachers. We could take advantage of that situation by giving students a leading role in sorting out how the technologies they know and like could serve the cause of their learning as well as the important goals of schools. This approach to technology would avoid both the dangers described earlier—of either overemphasizing technology or, alternatively, of forcing students to "power down."

What is increasingly clear, as a recent study put it, is that "technology serves at the pleasure of instructional design, pedagogical approaches, and teacher practices" so they are only valuable insofar as they support instructional goals (Tamim et al., 2011, p. 17). If we begin with good teaching and learning practices that engage students, then information technology can be a useful adjunct. Schools can support students and teachers in using various technologies to attain well-defined curriculum goals, but technology should not be the starting point.

INDEPENDENT LEARNING

When I was a young school board member in the early 1970s, our district sent a delegation to Calgary, Alberta, to look at Bishop Carroll High School. Bishop Carroll was well known as a school in which there were virtually no classes. Students developed individual learning plans with teachers, worked primarily on their own, and got assistance from teachers when they needed it. The school worked very well for those students who chose it and had very good outcomes. However, neither our district, nor the hundreds of other districts that visited, adopted the Bishop Carroll model. Bishop Carroll (searchable on Wikipedia) is still using this approach 40 years later; despite thousands of visitors, it remains highly unusual across Canada and the United States.

It is an irony that although one of the main espoused purposes of schooling is to create independent and lifelong learners, there is remarkably little independent learning in high schools. Increasing the amount of learning students do outside of or instead of scheduled classroom time seems a very desirable direction for high schools. Not only would it give tangible meaning to the goal of building independent learners, but it would also be highly consistent with the increased need for independent workers in the labor force and the world. It would have the further positive effect of reducing pressures on schools, especially small schools, to offer so many different courses because students could individualize their own studies. Insofar as some significant proportion of students could and would be working on their own, effective class sizes would be smaller, giving teachers more opportunity to work with students who need their support.

It is entirely reasonable to think that every high school graduate should have at least one significant independent learning accomplishment. Increased independent learning in schools could take several forms. Students could be encouraged to enroll in courses or programs that do not require physical attendance at a school or require it only some of the time. One avenue is through online learning. There are many online programs already available to support this kind of work, including virtual high schools across the world and postsecondary and skills programs that could connect to dual credits (described in the next chapter). All schools can offer opportunities for students to take one or more courses online.

Another option is for students to negotiate with teachers for arrangements in which independent learning is part of regular courses—by, for example, undertaking independent work instead of attending some classes. There are many students in high schools who could manage courses quite successfully without attending all classes; if this is arranged in advance with teachers, it will get a much better reception than it does now, when students unilaterally decide to miss some classes for whatever reasons, much to the annoyance of teachers. Students learn in this way to regulate their own effort and learning, as they will be required to do in universities and in many workplaces.

Further, a student who spends a summer studying archaeology, working on a forestry project, or learning about child care while working at a camp is also developing real and important skills and knowledge. Students should be able to get appropriate recognition for real knowledge and skills, regardless of where these were acquired. Typically referred to in the higher education world as Prior Learning Assessment and

Recognition, PLAR policies exist in some school systems but are rarely used. Secondary school systems could be much more active in this area by designating a whole range of areas in which students could have outside skill and knowledge evaluated for school credit. The most compelling examples include the following:

- Knowing how to read, write, and speak a second or third language
- Developing a particular skill, such as music, art, a sports skill, or a craft
- Knowledge obtained from self-study of something of special interest, such as the deep knowledge some young people acquire about some period of history, place, technology, ethnic group, or occupation

There are many community resources available to foster and support this kind of independent learning, which has the additional advantage of connecting schools to their communities. For example, students could study and write about local history or study a local industry.

Standards and processes need to be in place to make sure that independent learning is substantial and meaningful, but care must be taken that the process of recognizing independent learning is not excessively bureaucratic or difficult; the goal is to support and recognize such learning, not to make it difficult to get the recognition. Schools have a natural desire to have students gain all their credits at the school, not outside it, so the larger system (the district or state) may also need to play a role in establishing the kinds of learning that can be recognized and making sure that students are being encouraged to do independent work, not hampered from it.

Independent learning is not a panacea. Many students engaged in it will continue to require and want some adult support. Independent learning is not a matter of cutting students loose to sink or swim. However, the support for students in these modes is likely to be less intense than having students in a class all the time. There are quite a few schools across the United States that have figured out the system design and workload implications that provide teacher support to students without increasing overall demand on teachers.

To conclude this chapter, I have two more points. First, everything a school does should reinforce the importance of high expectations for students. High expectations are connected with more intellectual demand, more support for independent learning, and higher feedback and formative assessment value. Where expectations are low, the investment of both adult and student time and energy is also likely to be low. Expectations do not exist in a vacuum; they are interactive with performance, so as students show that they can do more, expectations—their own as well as those of the adults around them—are likely to increase further.

Finally, I want to say a word on testing, teaching, and learning. Assessment is one of the powerful forces that could be used to shape teaching and learning in high schools. For both teachers and students, much of high school is about getting ready for various tests and exams. The current climate of accountability, often connected to serious consequences for both students and educators, has certainly increased that focus. Students and parents are also anxious about these matters, which may lead them also to be more conservative in their response to ideas for change.

It would be foolish to suggest that one can or should ignore these pressures. They are real and are not going to go away, even if one hopes that assessment and accountability policies can be more strongly aligned with good educational practices than is presently the case. However, one key function of leadership is to facilitate better outcomes in the school by encouraging discussion among students, parents, and staff about how the school can best manage testing and accountability pressures without sacrificing good educational practice. This has to be a subject of serious discussion so that everyone can see how there can be improvement without jeopardizing anyone's future. Fortunately, there is good reason to believe that student performance on high-stakes assessments will improve if the ideas in this chapter and book are put into place. Good educational practice is a better way to get improved student performance than the nostrums about drills, practicing former

---

Another Example

In this . . . high school, in which half the students were eligible to receive free or reduced-price lunch, student performance on authentic assessments was the highest of all the 25 highly restructured schools from which this case was drawn. In this school, mathematics and science instruction were integrated in[to] the same class, and student work was project-oriented . . . Students were assessed based on portfolios of work in a variety of subjects, and expectations for students took into account their progress as well as the levels of excellence they had attained. Moreover, students were expected to have mastered elementary mathematics and if they had not, a Saturday tutoring program was available to help them along . . . Key elements that supported a rigorous curriculum in a mixed-ability setting in this school were small classes (limited to 15 students), the supplemental tutoring program, a visionary leader who had selected a staff with congruent attitudes, and the opportunity to interview students prior to students' admission to the school. (Gamoran, 2009, p. 12)

---

exams, or endless reviews of the same concepts. The best way to get good results is to have caring schools with strong programs, strong community relations, and effective teaching and learning practices.

CONCLUSION

We began this chapter with a reminder of how difficult it is to change teaching and learning practices in high schools. However, there are ways to do this; the chapter outlined several. Schools and systems that focus simultaneously on collective learning by teachers, improving assessment practices, engaging students in their own learning, and increasing independent learning are on the right road to making their schools not only more effective but also more satisfying places for students and for educators.

Take-Aways

- The central goal of teaching and learning in all schools should be to engage all students in tasks that have a high level of challenge and therefore stretch their skills and knowledge.

- It is vital that students see their school experience as engaging and motivating so they put more effort into it.

- The most important single element is to have teachers work collectively on effective teaching and learning practices.

- Working on student assessment practices is often a good place to start the process of instructional improvement in a high school, as it is a common requirement across all grades and subjects. Good assessment practices are strongly linked to more effective instruction.

- Students can contribute a great deal to better teaching and learning if given the opportunity to provide real input.

- High school students should do much more independent learning, which would benefit both themselves and the school. Information technology can assist in this effort.

CHAPTER SIX

Connecting With Community

The evidence on the enduring effect of outside factors on school outcomes is consistent and powerful. Socioeconomic status (SES), whether family income, parental occupation, or other measures, remains the single strongest predictor of education outcomes in most studies. Ethnicity, culture, and language can also be important correlates of life outcomes, though they often link with socioeconomic status; for example, some ethnic groups are typically less well-off or less successful than others. Nor is it just the socioeconomic status of individuals that matters; there is substantial research showing that the neighborhood or wider community also has an effect. That is, a student growing up in a better neighborhood is likely to have better school outcomes than a student of similar background and ability growing up in a very poor neighborhood (Organisation for Economic Co-operation and Development, 2010b).

By the time students reach high school, they are no longer living primarily in their families' immediate ambit; their lives are wider now, inevitably bringing them into contact with the life of the community around them for better and worse. Educators working in high-poverty or other challenging communities are well aware of the potential effect of that broader community on their students, from fewer opportunities for sports to the prevalence of crime and gangs. Moreover, schools are supposedly preparing students for this larger life. Could one conceive of a good education that did not include assisting students in making their way in the wider world socially, economically, and politically?

All this means that the success of high schools is inextricably linked with schools' ability to connect with families and the broader community. These connections happen in multiple ways but must be deliberately built. The chapter will illustrate some of the forms these connections can take. Many of these connections must occur at the district level or wider, which reinforces the central theme of this book that improvement is not just a matter of what individual schools do but must also involve systemwide efforts.

The ideas in this chapter are not new. Indeed, stronger connections between high schools and families, employers, or postsecondary institutions have been advocated many times by various reports and commissions. The fact that these recommendations are still not generally in place means that they are hard to do and won't happen without specific attention and effort.

The central goal of all this work is to have *schools that are deeply rooted in and connected with their local and broader community,* such that the boundary between the school and the community is hard to define in a clear way because the two are so interconnected.

Community is given a wide definition in this analysis. To be sure, it includes parents and families of students, but it extends beyond that as well to at least three other elements of the community. One of these is community organizations of various kinds, such as churches, ethnic associations, sports organizations, and the like. A second important element in any community is its employers and businesses. The third key component is the postsecondary sector: colleges, universities, and other educational organizations. Each of these elements requires attention in its own right.

It is important to remember that communities are sources of positive resources as well as potentially negative influences. There is a natural tendency, especially in high-poverty communities, to overemphasize the problems and underestimate the positives in the setting, since we tend to see the things that cause problems whereas influences that prevent problems or promote positive outcomes are often invisible. For this reason, it is common (though often incorrect) for educators to see their community as insufficiently supportive and many parents as insufficiently interested in their children's welfare. Every community, no matter how distressed, contains many hardworking people with positive attitudes who can serve as potential mentors and role models for students. Every community contains at least some institutions, whether religious bodies, sports organizations, music groups, or others, that provide worthwhile opportunities and resources for students. So one main challenge for schools is, as the song says, to "accentuate the positive, eliminate the negative, and latch on to the affirmative" in regard to the local community.

This is not an argument for failing to face the very real problems of many communities, which include lack of employment, poor housing, high crime rates, insufficient recreation, or other problems. These challenges are all too real and can be highly distressing to students and to schools. But as in everything else related to education, a clear-eyed understanding of the problems should never lead to despair about what can be done. These challenges may temper our approach and change timelines, but they do not change ultimate objectives.

WORKING WITH PARENTS AND FAMILIES

Much has been written about the way schools build strong, positive relationships with parents and families. Where alignment exists between schools and parents, student success is more likely; this is what Peter Coleman (1998) called "the power of three." There is a large body of research on parent involvement and engagement in education, although much of it relates to younger students (Harris & Goodall, 2008; Henderson, Mapp, Johnson, & Davies, 2007; Jeynes, 2010; Pushor, 2010). The scope of this book does not permit anything like a full discussion of this issue, but a few key lessons from many years of research are worth repeating:

- Parents and families universally want their young people to have good and successful lives, though they may vary quite a bit in their capacity to help their children attain these goals. Schools should always start with the assumption that parents, under the right circumstances, want to be allies in the welfare of students. Where this is not happening, problems often are caused by a difference in perspective and breakdown in communication.

- Studies of teenagers show that they continue to regard their parents as highly influential people and pay a lot of attention to what their parents think and the models their families provide.
- Parents and family members know a lot about their children, including many things that educators do not know. Because students can behave quite differently in various settings, teachers and parents may begin with divergent views about who a student is. (My mother reported being startled with the very positive view a first grade teacher took of one of my brothers, given her own very different experience with him at home.)
- Many parents are afraid or resentful of the school, especially if their own school experiences were not happy. Fear and resentment can explain many negative behaviors, including ignoring the school or acting aggressively.
- While parents want schools to pay attention to the individuality of their children, schools and teachers must think about all students and are therefore necessarily drawn toward some uniformity of treatment. Inevitably, the views of schools and parents will occasionally be, as Sarah Lightfoot (1978) described them, "worlds apart." Some tension is inevitable.
- Good relationships begin with respect. Where schools treat parents respectfully, even when there is disagreement, there is a much greater likelihood of developing effective relationships. This is particularly the case when cultural differences lead to very different ideas by students, families, or the school about what is acceptable behavior.
- Building relationships requires trust, which only happens with effort over time. People can change their attitudes and behavior but typically do so only slowly and with continued effort.

We also know that most parents do not want to be involved in running the school—though they may certainly have views about particular aspects of the school. Parents' main concern is to help their children be successful. Research suggests this is most likely to happen when home and school cooperate in holding high expectations for students' goals, effort, and performance; when there are common messages about what is required to be successful; and when there is ongoing, respectful, two-way communication. Schools often want to tell parents what they should do, but that can only happen when the school is also listening thoughtfully to what the parents think and believe.

There is a rich literature full of specific suggestions about how schools can connect more effectively with parents. In their discussion of home involvement, Balfanz, Bridgeland, Moore, and Fox (2010) offer a number of practical suggestions:

> Parent engagement strategies [are] based on research of what will meaningfully engage them. Such practices should be responsive to cultural differences and include prompt notification of academic, behavioral, attendance, or other problems; earlier contact throughout middle school and in and beyond . . . [high school] on what constitutes success in high school, a single point of contact at the school; information on high school graduation and college admission requirements, including financial aid and assistance every step of the way in negotiating the roadblocks on the way to college; individualized student plans; homework hotlines; access to learning centers within schools; and flexible schedules for parent-teacher conferences. (p. 17)

Many other suggestions have also been made, such as providing translation and interpretation for parents who do not speak the language of the school, making home visits to understand students' home lives, making regular contact with parents to share positive news about students, providing opportunities for parents to develop relevant skills (literacy, for example), and so on. No school is likely to do all or even most of these, let alone the many other ideas one can find in the literature (we later discuss issues of prioritizing among ideas and interventions), but virtually every option here would be useful in at least some settings. Much will depend on an understanding of the specifics of each school or district—who the students are, who the parents are, and what are the most important issues in a particular setting at a particular time—and then learning from evidence and experience which approaches produce the best results. The main point is to see parent engagement as a priority that requires time and attention.

It is often said that parents of high school students are less interested in participating in the school and the students are less interested in having them there. But what is clear from much evidence is that parents never lose their desire to see their children do well and be successful and that they overwhelmingly understand how important high school graduation is in that process. Parental engagement in secondary schools needs different strategies, but it is no less important.

As in so many areas, students themselves are a main resource for engaging parents, serving as essential go-betweens and translators as well as prime motivators for parents to participate in school events. Parents may not come to school to hear about problems with their children, but they may do so for events that show off their children's talents and activities. Similarly, events that involve food or build connections among parents themselves are also potential winners, especially in the early stages of building parental support. Moreover, bringing parents together has another important benefit. It builds connections in the community, thus increasing overall social capital. The more people in a community know each other, the stronger that community is in looking after all its children. Increased social networks are also powerful levers for reducing isolation, depression, and feelings of helplessness; people in groups feel stronger and more efficacious. Schools can play an important role in building that social solidarity.

Challenges to Community Engagement

A main problem for schools in regard to parent and community engagement is that it is typically an add-on to the jobs of already-busy people. As with anything that one wants to do in an organization, success is more likely if someone has that particular function as a priority but much less likely if that activity depends on someone having extra time or energy. This issue will be discussed further in Chapter 7.

Further challenges lie in the gap in understanding and experience that often exists between schools and their communities, especially in the communities where graduation rates are now lowest. These arise from differences between school staff and the community in backgrounds, cultures, and experiences, with the consequent danger of making incorrect assumptions about each other—with "those parents don't care about their kids" on the one side and "those teachers don't care about our kids" on the other.

The real challenge in working with parents and community groups, though, is conflict. The reality is that parents and other community members will not always agree with what the school does or wants. Parents are—and should be—advocates for their children. It is their job to take their kids' side most (if not all) of the time. Schools should understand this requirement rather than blame parents for it. In poor communities, where parents and community leaders see their children at risk of failure, parents may become angry with schools and accuse them of failing to provide what their children need. Those criticisms can be harsh, with schools and educators being accused of racism and other forms of bias. Where children are concerned, people can and should get very worked up! Dennis Shirley (2008) and Jeannie Oakes, Michelle Renee, John Rogers, and Martin Lipton (2008) are among those who have explored the ways in which community organizations have challenged school practices, sometimes with significant levels of conflict and often with positive results for children.

Still, people tend to dislike conflict; nobody wants to be accused of disinterest, let alone racism. This is one powerful reason schools are often reluctant to take on active community engagement. It takes a great deal of courage to invite a group of people to tell you what they think when what they think could be highly unflattering to your work. Yet this kind of airing of emotion is necessary to build productive partnerships. It is part of what it means to work with people respectfully. Educators should not be subject to abuse any more than students or parents should, but in areas where people care deeply, some emotion is unavoidable.

Conflict management skills can be very useful in these situations. There are well-known ways to handle situations of high conflict that people can learn. Many school leaders would benefit from some training in conflict resolution skills. The good news is that if one has confidence to work through the challenges, initial conflict can often turn into productive and trusting working relationships. Just as a group of angry parents can create great difficulty for a school or system, a group of positive parents can be a powerful ally in generating overall public support and resources.

WORKING WITH COMMUNITY GROUPS

Every community has a range of organizations that are potential sources of support for students. These organizations include churches or other religious institutions, youth clubs, ethnic associations, sports groups, and others. Many high schools exist in splendid isolation from these groups, not even knowing who they are let alone working with them to build bridges and provide support for students. This is particularly the case in urban areas or in challenging neighborhoods where few staff live nearby.

Although for some the term *community groups* is synonymous with nonprofit organizations, local business and employers are also an important part of the community and should be fully included in building school-community relationships. These links matter because young people live and, in many cases, will continue to live in these communities, shop or work in those businesses, and live out their social lives in those gyms, libraries, restaurants, and clubs. Young people are interested in the overall life of their neighborhoods. And as with parents, building connections with employers and workplaces also builds social capital in the community, with lasting benefits that go far beyond the school.

A good starting point, then, is an inventory of community organizations—who they are, what they do, which students are connected to them, and how the school might partner with them. The easiest way to produce such an inventory is to ask students to list the groups or organizations they know about. Indeed, this kind of community mapping can be a valuable part of a social studies or related class. Another useful activity can involve students giving the staff tours of the community as the students see it, including places that are safe and places that are less so.

Some of the most successful cases involve situations in which the schools are part of a broader coalition of community organizations that all work together on behalf of families. The Boston Compact is one long-standing example, but more recently, Cincinnati, Ohio, has developed another example of a system with some significant success using the same approach (Kania & Kramer, 2011).

In Cincinnati Public Schools, Community Learning Centers (CLC), act as hubs for community services, providing access for students and families to health, safety, and social services, as well as recreational, educational, and cultural opportunities. CincyAfterSchool is another youth development network that provides after-school academic and enrichment programs for students, in partnership with organizations such as the YMCA, the Urban League, Families Forward, and the Boys and Girls Club.

Programming In and With Communities

There are many ways in which community groups can support school programs and student education. Again, which particular dimensions are most appropriate depends on the situation and possibilities in each school, district, and community.

- Interesting adults can be brought into the school in various capacities. Community groups may have adults who can serve as mentors to young people. In some cases, these mentors will be able to build connections that are not possible within the school. Even very troubled communities contain adults who can be good role models and mentors to students, and many community organizations will have links outside the local neighborhood as well. This kind of mentoring can work especially well for students who do not feel fully included in the school—for example, minority groups that make up only a very small part of the student body and may not be represented on the staff at all. However, like anything else, mentoring works best when it is carefully planned and well organized (Society for Research in Child Development, 2010).
- Young people can learn more about the kinds of lives adults lead, including (but not limited to) their careers. To have local people talk about their work, the history of the community, or the cultures and customs of different groups can be a valuable educational experience.
- Community groups can provide settings for relevant learning experiences for students, whether these involve social studies, language learning, volunteer work, or other activities. Students not only get valuable experience, but they—and the school—can build contacts that can serve as the basis for other opportunities. School assignments can

require students to gather information about their own community, from studying its economic base to considering local health and pollution to using local lives as the basis for learning about local history. Virtually every secondary school subject could have some component of local community included, which is an opportunity that is often missed in favor of abstract representations through books. (As an instance, I once found my daughter studying a map of our area and learning the features by rote for a test without ever realizing that the river on the map was the same one that ran very close to her school.)

- Community groups can enrich school programs by providing opportunities for other important activities that schools may not be able to provide on their own, such as sports or a foreign language or art from a particular ethnic community.

- Communities are particularly important for assisting with career development activities for schools, since they are the places where most students will live and work after school. Career development activities, an important part of every secondary school, can involve many community connections such as cooperative education, work experience, job shadowing, or apprenticeship. Since most people get employment through networks of contacts rather than formal application processes, the more different people that students meet, the more opportunities will be open to them in future.

An Example of Community-Based Learning

The Long Beach Linked Learning Program transforms students' high school experience by bringing together several different programs:

- Challenging academics for college preparation are studied through a real-world profession.

- Technical skills that link academics with a professional career are taught through hands-on classroom work.

- Work-based learning is focused on a continuum of experiences ranging from career awareness and exploration to actual career preparation.

- Student support is provided through mentoring, tutoring, career counseling, and family support services.

WORKING WITH POSTSECONDARY INSTITUTIONS

Postsecondary education is important for all young people, and as it becomes an increasingly common standard for good jobs, high schools are devoting more attention to making sure all students are ready for postsecondary education. Some of the complications of that goal for high school curricula were discussed in Chapter 4. However, another option for schools is to build stronger connections with postsecondary institutions. Indeed, such connections should be a fundamental element in a program to increase high school student success.

There are several ways in which schools can work with postsecondary institutions. The main goal of these efforts is to give students more knowledge about postsecondary education so they can make more informed decisions about their futures. Clearly, students whose parents attended college or university are more likely to attend themselves. Though the reasons for this relationship are not one-dimensional; more knowledge about that world will encourage at least some students to take part in it.

One simple option is to schedule visits for students to colleges so they get a better sense of what such places are. Given that many students may never have been on a postsecondary campus and may not know anyone who has attended a college, just providing some familiarity is itself useful.

Another option is to share facilities. A nearby college or university might have a gym, studio, pool, or some other facility that is not in use full-time and could be made available to the high school. Sometimes high schools have facilities that postsecondary educational institutions can use. Bringing postsecondary and high school students together helps high school students understand more fully what postsecondary education is about.

Colleges are also good sources of potential mentors or role models for students and sometimes for volunteers for the school. College students are often interested in volunteering and can be effective tutors or other supports for high school programs. These kinds of contacts provide high school students with the opportunity to meet others only a few years older who have experienced success and who can give them suggestions that they would not accept from teachers or even parents.

However, the most important connections between schools and postsecondary institutions should be programmatic ones in which students use the resources of the postsecondary sector to support their educational goals. The most direct way to do this is through some variant of dual credit or postsecondary option programs, in which high school students take courses that count as high school credits and can also be used later as college credits.

Dual Credit and Early College Programs

Various forms of dual credits or postsecondary options have now been operating in various parts of the United States for more than 20 years. Tens of thousands of students have benefited from them (National Center for Education Statistics, 2005; National High School Center, 2007). There are many different models for such programs. Students can take part in individual courses or entire programs. These can be delivered in high schools or on college campuses. Instructors can be high school or college teachers. Various arrangements have been made for tuition and other costs: sometimes students pay them, sometimes the school pays, and sometimes the college absorbs the cost because these courses are great recruitment tools. The important point is that students get access to postsecondary courses and get a sense that postsecondary education is a real possibility for them.

The Bill and Melinda Gates Foundation has supported a great deal of this work in the United States. They support not only dual credit programs but also an exciting idea called "early college high schools" in which it is expected that most students, even those in highly disadvantaged communities, will not only complete high school in a timely way but also will gain at least some college credits as part of that process. Jobs for the Future (jff.org) has done much of the operational work, and their website contains many resources, examples, and evaluations of these programs. Many of these programs have been evaluated and have been found to be both effective and cost-effective (Hoffman, 2005; Webb & Mayka, 2010). Their effects are also long-term. Insofar as they change students' aspirations, they can improve not only the lives of students themselves but also the lives of those students' families and, in the future, their children's lives.

Still, after all these years and with so much supporting evidence, most dual credit or early college programs remain rather small scale. The model is far from universal, either across districts or within schools. Yet it seems entirely reasonable to think that at least 25% of students should take at least one dual credit course during their high school years; it would even be plausible to aim for 10% or more of all students to gain at least an entire year of postsecondary credit while still in high school. After all, the boundary between those two sets of institutions, though sharply demarcated, is really quite arbitrary. There are clearly many high school juniors and seniors who could do college-level work. Efforts in the United States to develop P-20 models, which would build a more integrated system from preschool through college, received much attention a decade or so ago but seem to have died away more recently; dual credit provides a simpler and more direct alternative.

The dual credit model should not be restricted to the strongest academic students. Ontario has had years of experience putting disengaged and unsuccessful high school students into technical programs in community colleges, with quite a bit of success (Canadian Council on Learning, 2008). Students who were not performing well in high school, when put into a different environment that fits more with their plans and sense of self, raise their level of performance quite dramatically. For example, in one study, high school students taking college courses not only exceeded their previous high school achievement, they outperformed regular college students in the same courses (Whitaker, 2011).

There is a strong incentive for postsecondary institutions to partner with such programs—namely, the opportunity to recruit students. A student who already has course credits at a particular institution is more likely to enroll there full-time after high school.

Dual credits can also provide an alternative to Advanced Placement and International Baccalaureate programs that many schools struggle to offer. In comparison with these stand-alone programs that place new demands on schools, dual credits can be more inclusive of all students and less expensive for schools to operate.

LEARNING ABOUT WORK AS A SCHOOL AND COMMUNITY FUNCTION

Preparation for employment is a central purpose of high schools, even though that purpose takes on varied meanings. For a significant number of students, the workforce will be their immediate post-high school destination, either for a short or long time. But even for those with high aspirations for college education and select careers, schools play an important role in their understanding of what work is and what it means. After all, the great majority of high school students in North America already work while in school and they all know that at some point in the future they will have to earn a living. Students overwhelmingly want to know about work and what it may mean in their lives.

While some commentators decry the focus on preparation for work as detracting from the other, loftier goals of education, such as citizenship or an appreciation for the finer things in life, in my view there is no contradiction at all between all these important goals. Work is a central part of almost everyone's life. Learning about work involves not only pleasing an employer but also developing a sense of who one is, what one enjoys and is good at, and how one's livelihood affects the larger community. Moreover, the skills that are seen as essential for many jobs (such as initiative, teamwork, or independent learning) are, to an increasing extent, also the skills and dispositions necessary for participating effectively in democratic civil life.

Schools have often had a narrow view of what is meant by education for and about work, seeing it as training people for particular occupations. There is good reason to be cautious about training in high schools for specific occupations, unless there are firmly established connections between the schools and the labor market. A recent OECD review of vocational education in schools (2010a) found that where school programs were highly integrated with workplaces and employers, such as through formal apprenticeship models, they could be highly effective, but when such links were absent, the prospects were much less effective.

All of this means that education for and about work involves much more than training people for particular occupations.

Indeed, as noted earlier, specific occupational training has not had much success in North American schools and has been linked with programs for the most marginalized students, leading to poor outcomes, and so is probably one of the least effective ways to help students.

Instead, school systems can think about education for work in a much broader way that supports high expectations and a rich and broad curriculum. Some of the possibilities already being used in various places include the following:

- Considering the work implications of various subjects within the curriculum. Science students can learn what kinds of work various scientists do; the same is true of every subject area if one adopts a broad view of work as related to various disciplines. For example, history is used by journalists, politicians, lawyers, business managers, and many others beyond history teachers.
- Providing students opportunities to learn about work through cooperative education, internships, independent studies, and volunteerism. Such learning can translate into important intellectual activity about the way work is organized, its effects on people, its legal and organizational structures, and even the different kinds of mathematics that get used in different kinds of jobs.
- Linking students' part-time work back to the school's curriculum instead of treating it as an interference. Even the most menial work that students do brings them in contact with important issues of interpersonal relations, organizational behavior, psychology, and of course, economics.

More structured models also exist. One of these is the career academy, of which there are quite a few models (Grubb, 2011). The essential idea is that students take a package of courses, the content of which is adjusted to address a particular area of the workforce such as health care, tourism, or retail, and combine that with cooperative education or other work placement programs in that industry. Building on the U.S. experience, Ontario developed the specialist high skills major as a further iteration of the same basic idea.

The Ontario Specialist High Skills Major

As part of its effort to improve high school graduation rates, Ontario looked for a way to revitalize education for work without the pitfalls of previous vocational education programs, which ended up being streams for low-achieving students and had poor outcomes in terms of graduation and later employment. The result was the specialist high skills major (SHSM), launched in 2006 and growing rapidly since then.

The SHSM works like this:

- The Ministry of Education designates economic or employment sectors where employer groups have indicated an interest in working more closely with schools. There are currently 20 sectors, ranging from agriculture to arts to mining to sports to transportation. The employers certify that students completing this program will be seen as immediately employable in their sector. The program works with the main economic sectors in Ontario but can adapt to local or regional needs where there is a focus on one industry or employer.

- Schools or districts put together a package of courses that are aligned to the employment needs of that industry. This can include modifying some elements of existing courses but more often means changing the examples, assignments, and other aspects of the course to be directly related to the sector involved.

- Schools work with the industry to create co-op placements (for at least one course, usually two) for students. These count as compulsory credits toward graduation.

- Employers identify other useful training and certification that students can acquire as part of their program. For example, students in agriculture or horticulture can get their pesticide handling certification; others get certifications in CPR or worksite safety. The idea is that students will acquire other credentials that are useful in the labor market as part of their program.

Each program also has a postsecondary partner, usually an Ontario community college. Part of the program must include a bridge into postsecondary education, should students wish to pursue this after high school—either immediately or later. Usually this takes the form of a dual credit course or courses so that students, in addition to getting direct employment experience and related curriculum knowledge, will also see possibilities for more advanced studies in that field.

The SHSM thus has direct connections to employment, adapted curriculum for that field, nonschool certifications, work experience, and post-secondary options all built in. Students typically enroll in the program in their last two years of high school and can do so while still meeting all other requirements for entry into a college or university. Students who complete the program have a special notation on their diploma. Participation is voluntary.

The SHSM has been wildly popular. In its first year, the SHSM began with 27 programs involving about 600 students. In 2010–11, it has more than 1,000 programs in 530 schools (there are about 800 high schools in Ontario in total) with some 28,000 students—about 10% of all students in the relevant grades. The program primarily serves students who are not aiming for university. Within a few years, every high school in Ontario will have at least one SHSM program.

More information is available at www.edu.gov.on.ca/morestudentsuccess/SHSM.asp

CONCLUSION

Most educators recognize the vital importance of family and community to children's success, yet most schools and school systems are too preoccupied with the daily work of their institutions to give this area much attention. The reality is that a school will have a hard time being successful unless these connections are built and that they are most important in the most challenged communities and where the students face the greatest obstacles to success. The good news is that strong community connections can actually reduce resource demands on the school; this is an investment, whether of time or money, that can pay for itself many times over.

Take-Aways

- Building strong connections with local communities is important but underemphasized in most schools and school systems. Like any other priority, this work requires dedicated effort.

- Even highly stressed communities have many resources that could be used to support students.

- Strong connections can be built with parents, but this takes some dedicated work and an understanding that some conflict is inevitable.

- Many students, including those who are not performing well in school, can benefit from connections with postsecondary institutions, such as dual credit programs.

- Students are very interested in employment, whether part-time during school or full-time later in their lives. Schools can use this interest and students' work experience as a powerful educational device.

CHAPTER SEVEN

Implementation

Many books make proposals for change but say little or nothing about how to bring them about. Knowing what to do is important, of course, but knowing how to get it done is at least as important.

Implementation cannot be taken for granted for a moment. Coming up with new ideas and designing programs is exciting work, but without effective implementation these are of little value. There is a long history in education of what were thought to be great ideas that never had the intended impact because not enough attention was paid to the hard work of implementation. Indeed, education literature is strewn with the words *must* and *should* but often without any suggestion as to how the desired conditions can be achieved. The idealism is admirable, the lack of practicality less so.

In education, we often assume that implementation is primarily a matter of motivation. If we can just get people to *want* to do the right thing, good results will follow. Motivation is important, but it is not enough. People also have to know how to do something; will is one thing, but skill is another. I could ask readers of this book to find a new cancer treatment. You may be highly motivated to do so. But you have neither the skills nor the wherewithal to turn your desire into reality. Good education practice is also a technical skill, not just a matter of motivation, and even the combination of will and skill is not enough if there is no systemic support for improvement.

An essential characteristic of effective implementation strategies is that they are blame free. The point is to create real improvement for students. This can only happen when all the partners work together and that in turn requires building trust and mutual support. All of these are undermined when the discussion is about who is at fault instead of being about what everyone needs to do together to create improvement. Yet much of the education literature is about blaming someone for problems. It's the fault of bureaucracy, of teacher unions, of education schools (colleges of education), or of uncaring parents. It is a natural human tendency when things are not going as well as we wish to try to assign blame, but this tendency is completely contradictory to what good organizations do and to what school systems must do to be successful, which is to enlist everyone in the effort to do better.

This chapter briefly outlines the implementation strategies that schools and systems will need to put the ideas in this book into place and sustain them over time. A fuller discussion of these issues can be found in my previous book (Levin, 2008). Another excellent source, with many specifics about implementation systems, is Michael Barber's book on "deliverology" (Barber, Moffit, & Kihn, 2011).

Implementation is both a technical and a political activity. It is about creating the structures and systems to support improvement while also paying attention to the human factors that make change successful. In education, these include building and sustaining teacher morale, strengthening leadership and teamwork across the system, organizing effective professional learning, maintaining strong relationships with stakeholders, allocating resources effectively, and giving enough attention to internal and external communications. If those things are not done, improvement will not occur, because people will not accept it or not know how to put it into place.

RESEARCH, DATA, AND EVIDENCE

Before moving to the details of implementation, a few words need to be said about the role of research and evidence.

Schools and school systems should rest on principles of rationality. We want our choices and actions to be governed by the best available knowledge about what will help us achieve our goals. In reality, people often fall short of that standard. We are as much creatures of emotion as of judgment, and as various researchers have shown (e.g., Stanovich, 2005; Tavris & Aronson, 2008), our rational capacities are not as great as we tend to think. It is salutary to read some of the research showing how easily people are inclined to make poor judgments based on faulty evidence both to remind us of our own limits and to help us think about how to reinforce the role of evidence in our organizations.

That being said, research and evidence can and should play a more important role in secondary education than they usually do. All too often ideas are adopted in education because someone in a powerful position likes them whether or not they have any strong evidence to support them. Educators should be wary in particular of ideas being proposed simply because they worked in School or District X. There are many reasons a program or initiative can have effects other than the theory underlying it. For example, a new program may excite and energize people so that they work more effectively, it may attract more talented people, or it may come with extra resources of various kinds. For all these reasons, in order to have confidence in the evidence behind a program, one should see multiple instances of sustained improvement over time, in different places, and without large inputs of additional resources.

The truth is, few programs or ideas can meet that test. There is just not enough research done in the field of education to have good data on all or even most ideas that are being proposed. That is one reason that many literature reviews conclude that more research is needed. A few studies can be indicative but are unlikely to be definitive unless the results are very strong and consistent indeed, which is rarely the case.

This kind of uncertainty is what leads many educators to think that one can prove anything with research. The frustration is understandable but not correct. Over time, in most areas, and with enough evidence, a consensus will begin to emerge on some durable findings. For example, the assertions in this book about the importance of connecting with students, the negative effects of failure on subsequent performance, or about the small effects of changes in class size are supported by large and consistent bodies of evidence. One can point to many other instances as well. John Hattie's recent book, *Visible Learning* (2008), is an excellent review of bodies of evidence on many ideas about effective educational practices—some of which appear to be not very effective at all.

Given the uncertainties and the technical nature of many reports of research, how ought schools and systems find reliable evidence? In brief, they should use the same spirit of enquiry as is proposed for many other aspects of education. We delve into the evidence, see where it leads us, and then use our best judgment to sort out what to do.

Currently, most schools and systems are entirely happenstance in their approach to research. If someone reads about a new idea or runs across it at a conference, it is considered. If nobody happens to look at any evidence, then it plays no role. That is clearly an inadequate approach. It is one reason school systems are so subject to fads that take a lot of attention and energy yet come and go without making much lasting difference.

A first step, then, is for a school or district to put in place a process for learning about and understanding the research evidence. There are many ways this can be done (Levin, 2010). Often, researchers are available and interested in working with districts to assess the strength and direction of current evidence. In most school systems, a significant number of staff are engaged in graduate study and could do this kind of research review as part of a masters or doctoral program while receiving guidance from a faculty member. Another option is for any group that is working on some part of the strategy to do or find a research review to inform the strategy. If one starts to look, the Internet has a huge range of resources in the form of reviews and syntheses of research. It is a reasonable expectation that any initiative being promoted in a school should be able to cite the evidence behind it; a reasonable step is to make finding this evidence a normal and expected practice for all initiatives being proposed in schools and districts.

The same mechanisms can work at the district level; indeed, they are easier there because there may be more skilled people or more ability to build partnerships with university researchers, state agencies, or some of the many research intermediary organizations that are interested in connecting research to practice and policy in education.

Indeed, schools and districts would benefit greatly if they set out to build such relationships with researchers. Over time, the two would work together to bring evidence to bear more effectively on the work of the district, to build the skills in the district, and to find, understand, and share good evidence, and thereby contribute to a culture that uses evidence to inform judgment.

STEPS TO EFFECTIVE IMPLEMENTATION

An effective implementation plan has seven elements:

- A strong focus on a few clear priorities throughout the organization
- A widely understood and accepted plan
- Infrastructure and resources focused on the priorities
- Systems, structures, and processes to support the plan
- Dealing with resistance
- Monitoring measures of progress
- Extensive two-way communication

As with everything in this book, these elements cannot be left to chance. Each of them must be deliberately organized and monitored.

Focus

The first and most important requirement for effective implementation is sustained attention. Sustained attention means that someone—usually a group or team of people—is paying careful attention to what is happening in the school or district and is taking regular steps to make sure that intended changes and improvements are taking place. There is simply no substitute for this kind of attention and follow-up.

As an example, a recent study of successful secondary schools by Harvard University researchers (Harvard Graduate School of Education, 2010) concluded that

leadership teams succeeded initially because they used their positional authority effectively to jump-start the change process. Then they built trust. More specifically, they demonstrated commitment through hard work and long hours; they studied research-based literature to expand their knowledge and competence; they persevered to follow through on the promises they made; and they found ways to remain respect-ful of peers, even when asking them to improve their perfor-mance. In these ways, leadership teams earned the respect of their colleagues and the authority to push people outside their comfort zones.

This sense of focus and attention must start with the top leadership of the organization, be it school, district, or state. If the senior leaders in a system do not "walk the talk" by doing the things outlined in this chapter, then they cannot expect others to believe in their leadership. Senior leaders include not only princi-pals or superintendents but also the political leadership—school boards, state boards and governors, or ministers and premiers, depending on the political system. The combined commitment of political leaders and staff brings an extra strength and sustain-ability to any effort. This commitment must be much more than a matter of issuing declarations or writing inspiring messages, though those things may also matter, as outlined in the next few pages. Without political leadership and support, lasting improve-ment is much harder.

To be more than rhetoric, commitment must turn into an ongoing and relentless focus on a few key goals. Schools are asked to do many things. Most high schools have lots of ideas and initia-tives at the same time—this has been called the Christmas tree school because there are so many ornaments on it at any one time, though the overall effect is not very satisfying. It is common for the goal statement of a school or system to have a dozen or more goals with no prioritization among them. This cannot work; to have too many priorities is effectively to have no priorities. If everything is equally important, then nothing is truly impor-tant. So an essential task of leadership in any school or system is to remind people—in deeds as well as words—that there are, and can be, only a small number of top priorities. In my view, no organization can have more than two or three truly high-priority issues if it wants to have a real and sustained focus. This does not mean that everything else is unimportant, only that first attention has to go to a small number of things. In Ontario, for example, though there were many initiatives and areas of atten-tion between 2003 and 2010, it was clear to everyone that two of these were by far the most important—literacy and numeracy attainment in elementary schools and increased high school graduation rates. Everything else was a lower priority.

Important goals must be sustained over more than one year because virtually no significant issue in a school can be addressed in a meaningful way in only one school year. Schools or districts that introduce new goals every year or two are unlikely to make progress on any of them. The activities to achieve the goals can change over time, but the main goals must persist.

What does it mean to have such a focus? It means that these priorities permeate everything the organization does. They are the main focus of all internal and external communication so that everyone understands what they are, and people throughout the organization can see their role in achieving these goals. There are clear metrics for progress. The key issues get first priority on the organization's budget so that they are resourced adequately. They are the main subject of discussion on every important agenda, from board meetings to staff meetings so that they are constantly on people's radar. They are the central preoccupation of the organization's leadership group, even though there may be a key person with the most responsibility for each priority. Data are collected and analyzed so that there is constant monitoring of progress and adjustment of plans in the light of new developments. Also important is that the organization manages other issues and pressures so that they do not distract from the main goals.

These things seem easy to say, but they are very hard to do, which is why so many organizational improvement plans founder.

A Plan

One reason that vision statements so often remain words on a piece of paper is that there is no realistic plan to translate them into reality. *Realistic* is a key word here; school and district plans are often too ambitious and cover too much ground to have any real chance of being put into effect. A good plan is short, sharp, and focused. It is about setting out the goals and strategies clearly. A plan should mainly, though not entirely, focus on the key priorities. The goal of the plan is to give everyone in the organization a clear sense of what is most important, with everything else by definition taking second place (or even lower) in the organization's efforts.

Given this purpose, building a school or district plan should be an open and collective activity that involves input from many people across the organization, although a first draft should come from the organization's top leadership to show their commitment. People need to feel that they have a personal stake in the plan, and this is best achieved if they are involved in its creation. For example, although government often wants secrecy in its planning, while creating goals and strategy for the Ontario ministry of education in late 2004, we required that every single staff person in the organization be involved in at least one meeting that gave them an opportunity to comment on the document. We also shared drafts and ideas early on with our partner organizations, such as teachers, principals, and parent groups. The goal was to develop something that had widespread understanding and acceptance; this in fact happened, as the key elements of the plan were spontaneously adopted by people across the ministry and in the wider education sector. Without any mandating, the key goals of the ministry were rapidly assimilated by the system and are still dominant across the province seven years later.

While participation is important, creating a plan should be a quick process. Many organizations create long and involved planning processes. By the time the plan is done, there is no energy or enthusiasm left for putting it into practice. Keep in mind that having a plan is not the point; making it work is the point. Planning processes should be short and to the point as well as participative. The plan itself, as a document, should also be short. The longer it is, the less likely that it will be implemented. A few priorities and the main strategies to accomplish them can be described, even for a very large organization, in a few pages. There should always be a one-page version as well, preferably with some kind of graphic format so that people can easily see the main points and can put them up in their workspaces as a reminder.

It is also important to reduce anxieties about planning. As soon as new goals are announced, people will inevitably start to worry about the implications for them personally in terms of their jobs, status, and roles. So it is important from the outset for leaders to reassure people that the goal is minimum disruption to the organization and maximum focus on reaching the goals. A particular mistake that senior leaders make often is deciding to reorganize as a first step to a new plan or set of goals. But reorganization is often very costly in terms of time, energy, and morale as people are distracted from the goals, often for many months, by worrying about where they will fit in the new organizational model; often, the new organization is not much more successful than the old one. My approach to this is the aphorism that with the right people and culture, almost any organization can work, but no organization will work without the right people and culture. In other words, try to avoid large reorganizations.

Infrastructure and Resources

Even without major reorganizations, main priorities must be supported by clear responsibilities and adequate infrastructure. Educational improvement is about changing the way people behave every day. This is hard to do; human behavior patterns are deeply entrenched even when we do not particularly like them or find them effective. All of us regularly do things that we know are counterproductive, and we usually find it hard to change those things. In education reform, we often behave as if simply telling people to do something differently will produce the desired result. Most of the time, it will not. It is not possible to change practice for any significant number of principals, teachers, or students by providing a consultant, a day or two of professional development, and a few materials.

When the Blair government in England set out to improve literacy outcomes in schools, they hired 300 consultants to work with teachers, but even this number, given that there were 20,000 schools, proved too small. In Ontario, we created dedicated units to support districts and schools on our major priorities. The staffs of these units were highly skilled educators who were sources of support for schools rather than managers, accountants, or regulators, so these resources were not seen by the system as extra administration but as a vital part of the improvement process (Levin, 2008).

The creation of a support infrastructure is one way an organization mobilizes its resources to achieve its goals. In general, schools do not do this well. They tend to be organizations that keep budgets pretty much the same from year to year; any new initiative requires new resources. Schools do not typically think of their key resource, staffing, as one that can be allocated in more or less effective ways.

This topic could command a book of its own—and has. Norton Grubb's book, *The Money Myth* (2009), is an excellent discussion of the kinds of resources schools have, especially high schools, and ways in which they can be used more effectively. Grubb points out ways in which we allocate staff, organize professional learning, and build community as key aspects of resource allocations. He also makes the point that resources in schools work in complex ways. For example, skilled teachers are more effective in a school with good leadership and high collegiality. High levels of interpersonal conflict make everyone less productive than they would otherwise be.

Reallocating resources to key priorities also implies doing fewer other things. For example, in Ontario, some of the costs of the support infrastructure were lowered because of a large reduction in curriculum work. We reduced dramatically the amount and speed of curriculum change because of a belief that changing teaching was more important than producing new curriculum documents. We tried to reduce the demand for new special education services in order to focus more attention on daily teaching. Taking resources out of lower priorities also has the positive effect of reducing the number of initiatives people are working on, which further reinforces the priorities.

The main point is that there are important resource choices to be made in every school and district—about who will work on what issue, who will teach which classes, the mix of professional and other staff, how professional development time will be used, and so on. Resource choices are about much more than money; they are about how people work together and support each other. When put together intelligently, these choices can have very large impacts on what a school does and how successful it is.

Structures, Systems, and Processes

Things are accomplished in schools when someone cares about them enough to do the follow-up. The words and deeds of senior leaders are one way in which priorities are communicated, but they are not enough. Changes in organizations can only be sustained when the organization's structures and systems reinforce and support them. Too often, school system priorities are left to the energy of a few key leaders instead of being made part of the normal work of the organization. When those people leave or get tired, the new initiatives are lost. Compare this to the way that many routines, such as payroll, are done. Nobody thinks that the payroll will stop because the payroll manager has left. These issues get attention because they are embedded in the daily work of people, and there are regular systems and routines to ensure they get done.

Leaders need to pay attention to how their priorities are turned into structures and routines, whether they appear automatically on agendas of key meetings or are part of standard reporting. They then become part of everyday organizational life.

To ensure this attention is properly given, it is important to have a lead person designated for any issue that is considered a priority, so someone can give the file his or her full attention. Who that lead person is depends on the specific setting; leaders can usually identify people who are well suited to take on these leadership roles. It may be someone in an administrative position, or in a school, it may be a teacher or two. The important thing is to know that someone is giving their full attention to the goals of the schools and reminding others of how important they are as well as embedding them in the organization's routine work. Delegating leadership in this way also helps build a sense of distributed leadership in the organization so more people feel a sense of commitment and responsibility for the goals.

Strong leadership has to be combined with effective teamwork. If only one or two people in a school care about something, it cannot be sustained over time. So another key implementation task is to build a team of people who work together and support each other in achieving important goals.

Working in a good team gives everyone more energy. It distributes the work but also provides mutual encouragement and support. People can share ideas and solutions as well as frustrations, gaining ideas and energy from each other. For most of us, being part of a strong team is an intensely satisfying experience.

Teams also help break down the internal divisions within organizations and create greater coherence. A huge challenge in large organizations, such as states or districts, is their balkanization so that what one part of the organization does may contradict another part. Creating greater alignment across the organization is achieved in part through a shared plan and good resource decisions but even more through creating the kind of teamwork that brings people together in a common cause.

A school or district leadership team should involve a senior leader—such as a principal or vice principal in a school—and should include the person with designated responsibility for the issue. It should also reach out to others who may be interested, including teachers, students, support staff, or parents, since it is important to encourage and allow others to take on leadership roles. One of the worst problems of strong leaders is their desire (or sometimes need) to do too much themselves, thereby stifling (usually inadvertently) the leadership potential of others. While senior leaders must support the leadership team, they need not chair it and may not even play a particularly strong role if others on the team are able and willing to do so.

Dealing With Resistance

The challenge of building a team is managing those in the school or district who simply do not want to get on board. Every organization has resisters, but people show their resistance in different ways. Sometimes they are actively negative and hostile. Sometimes they are deeply committed to their own approach and afraid of losing something important—for example, they may fear that their subject area will become less important. Leaders should not take resistance personally or to think of it as an issue of authority. "They should do what I say because I'm the boss" is a poor rationale for any educational activity, because the essence of education is that people—students and parents as well as staff—should be thoughtful in their responses and choices.

Resistance sometimes needs to be ignored and sometimes needs to be confronted. Often if there is enough support for a new direction, it can be best to leave resisters alone while giving them opportunities to join in when they are ready. Peer pressure from other staff will often bring people in over time. In other situations, the best strategy is to engage actively—to try to understand why people don't agree and to address their concerns. Resisters may have valid concerns that need to be heard and that can make an initiative or strategy more effective when attended to. Enthusiasm for a plan or goal can blind us to important constraints, while listening actively to resisters can help us see and manage those constraints. Sometimes all people want is a real chance to be heard and to be met at least partway, after which they can engage with the larger effort. On occasion, giving someone with a different view a leadership role can work very effectively to bring them in.

Those are the positive options, but sometimes resisters are actively negative and act to sabotage efforts that most people in the organization want and support. In these cases, it is often possible to isolate or neutralize them—while also always holding the door open for them to rejoin the larger team. In my experience, it is necessary only on rare occasions to move someone out of an organization because their actions are simply too destructive to countenance. This should always be a last resort.

The best single remedy for resistance is success. When good things are happening in a school and when staff members see students achieving more success, it is very difficult for individuals to cleave entirely to a different route. One of the aphorisms I had as a basketball coach was "Winning solves most of your problems," and the same is true of other aspects of organizational life. People want to be part of success.

Indicators of Progress

Often, in schools our goals for improvement are vague, in which case it is very hard to know if we are making progress. Without some clear targets for improvement, it is impossible to know how we are doing. Key priorities and goals should have clear and measurable indicators of success so that everyone can understand how much progress is being made. For example, a goal could be to reduce the number of suspensions and at the same time reduce the difference in suspension rates among various groups in the school. Another goal could be to reduce particular achievement gaps by 25% over three years.

These targets need to balance ambition with realism. I have argued that we often underestimate what students can do with the right support, which suggests that we should aim high. But high does not mean impossible. A target of 100% proficiency is not realistic and so will produce cynicism. For most schools, it will be a real stretch to produce even modest sustained improvement over a few years.

Once there are goals, it is vital to collect data to see what progress is being made and to share that information broadly so that everyone can assess the progress.

Of course, one should never confuse a measure, especially a single measure, with the underlying goal. For example, one could conceivably reduce the rate of suspensions without actually improving the climate of the school. No measure is perfect; every measure has its limits and a certain amount of error. Many times in education, reaching a number in a plan becomes more important than the purpose that the number represents. Indicators are exactly that, so one must be vigilant that the indicators do not displace the actual goal. One solution to this challenge is to use multiple measures; this results in a picture that is more confusing to interpret but also one that is less likely to be abused.

A second concern is that reporting on progress is contentious in schools, with good reason. In too many cases, accountability systems have not been about understanding the barriers to progress but about assigning blame. Educators rightly resent it when goals are set unilaterally and then they are berated for failing to achieve them. If goals and progress are used for purposes of blame or punishment, they will be resisted. If they are used for purposes of rewards, they will be manipulated. Teaching test-taking skills to get better scores is not the point; helping students develop real skills is the point and insofar as the former contradicts the latter, policies that lead to more test preparation are bad policies. Leaders need to be alert to the possibility (indeed, the likelihood) that policies, especially in areas such as reporting progress, will have negative unintended results. Where such results are occurring, the policies usually need to change. Despite its problems, measuring progress remains an essential task.

Communicate Often and Openly

In virtually all organizations, one of the most frequent complaints of staff is inadequate communication with senior management. The goal of communications is dual—to tell people what is happening and to hear their concerns and ideas. In regard to the former, the goal is to give people a storyline that explains what the organization is trying to do and allows them to see how things are going and where they fit in the whole enterprise. In a successful organization, everyone has a shared understanding of these issues.

In today's electronic world, there is no excuse for having an uninformed organization. It is easy to send all staff and students regular updates on how things are going. This keeps everyone informed but also reminds people of how important the work is and helps establish a common culture. These updates can remind people of the goals and purposes, inform people of progress, reinforce success that will then foster further effort, and identify challenges. Regular, open communication is particularly important in creating a positive organizational culture and in squelching the rumors that may otherwise circulate. It is also a way in which leaders help staff make sense of change.

Communication does not only happen through vehicles like e-mails or newsletters. It is embedded in the day-to-day interaction among people. As mentioned, people in an organization watch their leaders closely for consistency between rhetoric and action. In every visit to a classroom, in every chat with a teacher or student, in every event in which they participate, leaders should be reinforcing their commitment (and thereby the commitment of others) to the goals of the school.

Communication also has to be two way. While it is important for the leadership to talk to the whole organization about what is happening, it is equally important to listen to and get feedback from others. Feedback is especially important when it is inconsistent with what the leadership thinks or believes. Herein is another dilemma: strong leaders have the courage and passion of their convictions, but they need to be especially attentive to others who do not share that passion, because that is the only way to see clearly some of the problems and challenges. One of the most important things leaders can do is to admit that a mistake has been made—to indicate that something has not worked as intended and will be changed. It is astonishing how much goodwill can be generated when the leadership is willing to acknowledge and respond to real concerns.

This kind of two-way dialogue benefits if it is institutionalized in some ways. Informal discussions are necessary, but as is so often the case, establishing structure helps ensure things get attended to. In Ontario, we set up several formal vehicles for consultations with stakeholders in addition to all the informal contact that took place. The minister created a partnership table that brought together more than 20 organizations on a regular basis to discuss and provide advice on important issues. Out of this came several working groups that gave more intensive consideration to areas of high importance, such as teacher development and special education. The result was a high degree of consensus on policies before implementation. These discussions continued after an announcement as well, so we could review progress and work with our partners to solve the problems that inevitably arose during implementation.

Open communication also means fewer things being mandated or made compulsory. In general, leaders should try to avoid compulsion in favor of building commitment. When priorities are built into organization routines and deeply understood by people, they do not need to be made compulsory and are far more likely to be sustained.

Communication must be external as well as internal. An essential point of this book is that school success depends on strong relationships with the broader community, and that relationship also requires extensive communication in forms that are appropriate to different audiences. Print materials may have to be translated into other languages and definitely have to be written in terms that can be understood by parents rather than the terms educators often use. Public events can also be used to discuss key priorities.

A final point about communication is that it is not the same as promotion or public relations. Here is a secret: the public already knows our schools are not perfect. A few more press releases or glossy brochures will not change their mind on this point. School systems can and should admit imperfections and challenges because the public, who pay the bills and send us their kids, are already well aware that these exist. When we are willing to be open about our limitations, others are more likely to believe in our good intentions and do their part to help. It is a natural tendency for organizations to want to put forward only good news, but in the long run only a more honest communication can produce real trust and partnership.

DISTRACTIONS

One of the most common complaints of leaders in education is that they end up spending too much of their time on things that are less important, so they don't have time for the things they really care about. Insofar as this book provides school leaders with even more things to do, it is likely to exacerbate the conflict between what people want to do and what they seem to spend their time actually doing.

To some extent, this mismatch is inevitable in any organization, since all organizations require significant attention to routines in order to continue. If people do not get paid because of an administrative error, they will not be disposed to accept the excuse that we were too focused on doing instructional leadership! Routines do matter, and routine matters do need attention.

That being said, it is possible for leaders to get closer to the kind of use of time that they regard as important and optimal. Skilled leaders do this repeatedly. Of course, even the most skilled leaders have their frustrations also, but they are somehow able to put the time into the things that matter to a larger degree than most of us.

A full discussion of how to do this would take more space than is available in these pages. However, I do have some suggestions to help school leaders keep the focus on what really matters:

- Determine the few critical things that must happen for your organization to succeed and that only you can do. By definition, those are the most important things for you to do. Build these tasks into your schedule first and protect them. If classroom or home visits are important, schedule them first and then try to fit everything else around them to protect that time, instead of waiting to find free time (which never happens) to do what's most important.
- One way to make sure your priorities become realities is to tell others that you have scheduled them. Set a public target for the number of visits you want to make to schools or classrooms, for example. When your commitments are public, you will be less inclined to cancel them due to last-minute pressures. This kind of public declaration can also provide a good reason to miss events or tasks given to you at the last minute by the head office.
- Hold fewer and shorter meetings. Eliminate discussion of things that can be communicated on paper or through e-mail and focus meetings on things that require group

discussion. If you have meetings on your schedule that you do not find useful, don't go to all of them, go late, or leave early. In most organizations, meetings are among the least productive uses of time.

- Delegate. The key goals of the organization need time, which means other things have to be done by someone else or done more quickly or to a lower standard. If leaders insist that everything be done the way they would do it, then they will end up doing everything themselves, and many important things will simply not be done. Getting something done at 80% quality is better than not getting it done at all while waiting to achieve 100%.

Most important in staying focused is constantly reminding ourselves of what really matters and asking how we can spend less time on the things that don't. As good citizens of an organization, educators often rush to do what others—staff, parents, or the head office—ask, even if it is less important, but the educators who are remembered and admired are those who had the courage of their convictions and the ability to keep their focus on the things that are truly important to student outcomes and to equity. Nobody wants to be remembered at retirement for getting all the transportation reports in on time and accurate to two decimal points!

The Seven Oaks School Division in Winnipeg, Canada, has been working on improving success in their high schools for a decade now. Over that time, they have gradually introduced a whole range of supports consistent with the ideas in this book:

- Each student has a single teacher advisor/advocate for his or her entire time in the high school who presents the diploma when that student graduates, which is often an emotional event for both student and teacher

- A partnership with the University of Winnipeg allows students to start taking university courses while still in high school, with a particular focus on Aboriginal and minority students

- Several school-within-a-school programs that allow a more tailored curriculum approach for particular groups of students

- A Bright Futures program provides extra support to students identified as needing it without slotting them into lower level courses

- Constant efforts to reach out to the community, including to Aboriginal and visible minority populations

- A strong student voice program involves students in school policy and community outreach

- An approach to transition so that when students arrive in high school they already have connections to the staff and program

- Constant efforts to help teachers improve their daily teaching practices

These programs did not happen all at once. The district began with a commitment to improvement, constant analysis, and discussion on what was working and adjustment for what was not. The school board, senior leaders, principals, teachers, support staff, students, and parents have all been directly involved in this work. The result is a district that is now above the provincial average for graduation, even though its student population has more challenges than the provincial average.

CONCLUSION

The essential point of this chapter is that one must give as much attention to the *how* of improvement as to the *what*. Improvement does not happen by itself. It has to be built and sustained carefully. Too often, education reforms are announced but never get the support and attention they need to take root and flourish, which leads to increased cynicism and disengagement by stakeholders. This is not inevitable, and the steps to prevent it are outlined in these pages. The most important step is paying attention.

Take-Aways

- The implementation of change is as important as its design but is often not given enough attention.

- Effective change begins with careful attention to the evidence on current results and possible improvements.

- A school or system can only focus on a small number of core goals; too many goals will lead to fewer changes.

- While a clear plan is important, do not spend too much time creating it.

- Change and improvement require dedicated resources, systems, and processes; they cannot be left to the extra efforts of a few heroes. This means designating people and teams to lead particular changes.

- It is vital to have good measures of progress.

- There is no such thing as too much communication about change; communication should be as positive as possible to build commitment and morale.

- Set up processes to reduce the impact of distractions so that the organization can stay focused on its key priorities.

CHAPTER EIGHT

Conclusion

In his 1971 book about schools and teaching called *How to Survive in Your Native Land*, James Herndon defined an institution as "a place to do things where those things won't be done." Herndon's point is that the weaknesses and failures of institutions are usually not the result of bad people or bad intentions; they are more often the result of inattention. Things slide gradually away from what we wanted or planned, and in the absence of strong action, they continue to move that way.

High school is a critical period in students' education and in their lives. These are the years that decide the future trajectory for many students, when they come to see themselves either as confident and competent learners or as having limited abilities and so limited futures. Success in high school and a good entry into work or postsecondary education is a base for many students' life journeys. These are also the vulnerable years of adolescence when students come to understand who they are as people and what degree of agency they feel they have over their own futures.

Because these years are so important to young people, what we do as educators matters enormously. Although educators sometimes talk as if students' futures are determined by their capacities and attitudes, it is clear that adults can have a huge impact on students' thinking and their lives. The research on resilience shows how important a single caring adult can be in helping a student. Most of us can remember a teacher who made a real difference in our lives by inspiring us, by giving us confidence, by pushing us to accomplish more than we ourselves had thought possible. Often, as shown in the short article titled "20 Minutes to

153

Change," even a small amount of time can make a big difference to a students' future.

---

20 Minutes to Change a Life?

Sometimes there is serendipity in the way an idea comes to us from several different places at about the same time, making it seem like something that really requires our attention. In the last couple of months I've had three different reminders of the difference that teachers can make to the futures of students, especially in high schools, and often with a remarkably small investment of time and effort. It seems that in many cases as little as 20 to 30 minutes of supportive adult attention can move a student from the wrong path to the right one.

My first encounter with this idea was in a conversation with Amanda Cooper, a high school teacher who is now a graduate student at OISE. She recounted talking with some colleagues about working with students in difficulty. At one point in their conversation she asked the group how much time they needed with a student to change that student's trajectory in the school from negative to positive. The group concluded that quite often 20 minutes of concentrated time with a student was enough to make a significant change in the student's attitude, outlook, and behavior.

Then, last March at the AERA conference, I heard a talk by Susan Nolen, a friend and professor at the University of Washington. She asks teachers working with her to spend 30 minutes out of class time—for example, over a lunch hour—just getting to know a student with whom they do not relate very well. She reports that the teachers overwhelmingly say that this simple step not only gave them a deeper and more positive understanding of the student, but often dramatically altered the way the student engaged in their class as well. Once students felt that the adults involved actually were interested in who they were, their willingness to make a positive contribution rose.

The third instance of the same idea was in the September, 2008 issue of Education Leadership. An article[1] on seeing the best in students cited work by Ray Wlodkowski about something he calls a "two by ten" strategy. The way this works is that for two minutes a day for 10 consecutive days, a teacher has a personal conversation with a difficult or challenging student about something the student is interested in. The authors report that this simple strategy will almost always yield noticeable improvement in the student's attitude and behavior in the class.

These are remarkably similar and remarkably encouraging conclusions. When evidence from different sources points in the same direction it increases confidence that the findings are truly valid.

Every time I share this finding with educators I get further confirmation. A high school principal in Winnipeg recently told me about their school's graduation, in which each graduate is asked to say something about him or herself. Very often graduates name someone—a teacher, a parent, or someone else—whose belief and support they felt was crucial to their success. "I could not have made it without *X*," is the typical comment. Occasionally it's the opposite: "This is to show Mr. *Y* that I can do it after all." Further reinforcement comes from studies showing how many adults, decades later, can recall, with considerable emotion, a remark made by a teacher that either was vital in encouraging them or, sadly, sometimes had the opposite effect.

All these pieces of evidence support a point that emerges powerfully from the research on dropping out of high school—that the single biggest factor in whether students try or give up, leave or stay, is their sense that somebody in the school knows who they are and cares about what happens to them. Study after study has pointed to the importance of those personal connections in giving students, especially those facing real challenges, the desire to persist.

These ideas put a new slant on the effort to improve high school success and graduation rates. Around the world, large-scale improvement has proved to be considerably more difficult in secondary schools than in elementary schools. There are good reasons why this is so, including the more complex organization of secondary schools, the division into departments and subjects, the different attitudes of secondary school teachers, and the multiple and inconsistent expectations for secondary schools. A few years ago the World Bank issued an excellent book on the challenges of secondary education[2] that also identified the contradiction between the role of schools in creating success for all, and their role in sorting students in terms of their destinations.

Raising graduation rates has proved to be a considerable challenge, though, for reasons just mentioned. The most prominent ideas advocated for high schools do not seem to work all that well. Creating new courses or programs for disengaged students runs the risk of relegating those students to tracks that are less desirable with fewer future options. Reorganizing high schools into smaller units, or creating teacher-advisor systems, has proved difficult to do and does not always yield the desired results.

How might a "twenty minute" view of the world inform the way we think about improving high schools? It would put our focus on the relationship between teachers (and other adults) and students, not in a mechanistic way but as people reaching out to each other. It would remind us of the importance of personal connections in the lives of students, and especially for those students facing the greatest challenges to their success.

Of course it's not as simple as finding twenty or thirty minutes for each struggling student. Sometimes twenty minutes will not be nearly enough, and many times one "dose" of attention won't be sufficient. Some students have challenges that are much more severe. Some students will test us as adults repeatedly, just to see whether our commitment is more than rhetorical. Some students will fall off the path repeatedly, and some will engage in behavior that no school can tolerate.

Moreover, caring itself is not enough. Students still need to develop real skills, and we do them no favor if we pretend otherwise. Schools will still have to pay attention to curriculum, pedagogy, and support services. Students need us to push them to do more and better work, to do and be more than they thought they might be capable of. This requires effective pedagogy, engaging curriculum, good assessment practices, outreach to parents and families, and opportunities for students to improve their skills and knowledge through practice and feedback. Here, as in every other area of education, there is no magic bullet for student success.

Still, the idea that there are many students for whom a single conversation, or 2 minutes a day for ten days, will make a real difference to their futures should give every educator pause. Our words and our attitudes to students really do matter! This should be an idea that is both exciting and frightening, since it speaks both to the impact and the responsibility of every educator. Who are those kids in our class and our school? How can each of us be confident that our interactions with students are moving them toward the right path? It's a question we should keep in our sights as we work with young people, with all their potentials, delights and frustrations, each day. (Levin, 2009)

Notes

1. Rick Smith and Marv Lambert. "Assuming the best." *Educational Leadership,* September, 2008, *66*(1), pp. 16–20.

2. World Bank. *Expanding opportunities and building competencies: A new agenda for secondary education.* (Washington, DC: World Bank, 2005).

Originally published in *Kappan* magazine, January, 2009. Reprinted with permission.

Real and meaningful human contact is the glue that holds schools together, but it is not enough in itself. A school is a place of learning as well as caring. As proposed in this book, improvement requires attention to all the key aspects of the organization's work. Schools need to know and care for their students, but they also need to offer good programs, connect with their communities, and focus on powerful teaching and learning practices. When all these things come together, the results can be impressive and can change the lives of many students.

In Ontario in 2011, nearly 20,000 more young people will graduate from high school than graduated six years ago. There is, of course, no guarantee that graduating will solve all their problems or grant them a good life. There are no guarantees in life of any kind. But we do know that failing to graduate would greatly increase the likelihood of poor life outcomes, less employment, lower earnings, poorer health, and a shorter life span. Completing high school is for most young people today a starting point for building a good life. The better that education is, the stronger the foundation they have.

The journey to institutional improvement is necessarily long and challenging. Glossy reports from various places may show charts with steady upward lines, but in most cases, reality is a jagged line, which has drops and plateaus even in the process of improvement. Not everything will go as planned. Some ideas will prove to be dead ends. Some programs will not work or will work only temporarily. Important people leave the organization, and new ones have to be brought up to speed. Progress is often a case of two steps forward, one step back.

This means that those who set out on the journey of improvement have to be in it for the long haul and able to tolerate the inevitable setbacks and moments of disappointment and disillusion. It is critical to include people and build teams, because no individual (or even small group) can do all that is needed. It is important to set up systems, structures, and processes to support improvement, because these are the best guarantees of long-term attention, even as people change. It is important to have good data on progress, because nothing builds lasting commitment more than success. As people see good results from their work, they are encouraged to do more of it. For adults and students alike, success is addictive—in a good way.

While improvement is a long-term venture, one does not need to wait forever to see any results at all. School improvement can generate good results in the very short-term—within one school year—even if the whole strategy is not yet in place. When a school truly becomes a place that welcomes and values students and is interested in their development and success, results will improve—sometimes dramatically.

Good improvement work requires a balance between patience and impatience. One must be impatient to see good results. Students only get one chance at a good high school education, so every year, every month, and every day matters. Recognizing that change takes time does not mean one should be any more accepting of lags than is absolutely necessary. I remember one group of teachers telling me that their only regret on their improvement journey was that they did not start sooner and move faster, because looking back, they feel guilty about the students who could have had those benefits but did not. Regularly remind everyone involved that, as my colleague Avis Glaze, Ontario's first chief student achievement officer, used to say, "The kids can't wait."

Optimism is another key quality for anyone involved in school improvement. Optimism and confidence are contagious, as is pessimism (in the wrong direction). Optimism does not imply blindness to reality or the overlooking of real barriers; it does imply a confidence that continued effort will yield continued results. It also serves to get us through the days when not everything is going well or according to plan.

When a commitment to good student outcomes is coupled with a good sense of strategy, is well grounded in evidence, and has a strong commitment to effective implementation, the results will almost always be good—often surprisingly good. High schools will never be perfect and will probably never even be as good as educators want them to be. But they can, without a doubt, be better than they are today. And that idea is what this book is intended to promote.

Epilogue

When I showed a draft of this book to my friend and colleague Michael Fullan, he advised me to add an epilogue as a call to action. As readers finish this book, I hope you will keep these key points in mind:

1. We can do better in our high schools. Despite all the pessimism about past efforts, we do know quite a bit about how to make high schools better places of learning for young people, leading to more of them developing the skills and knowledge they need for life and so being able to graduate and go on to do other worthwhile things. We also know that young people are virtually always capable of more than we or they think and that with the right supports and motivation, almost all of them can reach levels of achievement they would have thought impossible.

2. We have to act—now. We will never have all the answers, and as Fullan (2008) has pointed out, much of the best learning comes from implementation. Even the best-performing schools and systems could be better still. All leaders in education have to work to create and support systemwide improvement in our high schools. This is absolutely urgent and has to be felt as such.

3. There are no silver bullets. Do not waste time thinking that adopting a single program or model or policy, whatever it is, can create the significant improvement that is needed. There is no way forward other than a thoughtful and comprehensive strategy, followed by the hard work of careful implementation sustained over years. To suggest anything else is a confidence trick.

4. Any system can implement the basic ideas in this book: the four clear areas of focus, the commitment to an open and positive process of improvement, and the effort to help everyone get better at their work. Although policies and funding at other levels of the system can help (or hinder) the work, there is nothing to stop

any school, district, state, or other system from acting now on these ideas. Start where you can, go as hard as you can, and other things around you may also change to make the work easier and even more successful.

5. Everyone has a role in this work. Yes, leadership matters, a lot. But excellent leaders know that they are only as successful as the people they work with. In education, this means working with and respecting teachers, support staff, parents, and most of all, students as the people who will make improvement happen. As the Chinese sage Lao Tzu wrote in the *Tao Te Ching* nearly 3,000 years ago: "If you don't trust the people, they will become untrustworthy. The best leaders value their words, and use them sparingly. When the task is accomplished, the people say, *Amazing: we did it, all by ourselves!*"

6. We need to combine, as Collins (2001) argued in *Good to Great*, passion with humility. We have to believe utterly in the value of what we are trying to do while simultaneously—and this is the trick—recognizing that we do not know everything and that we are going to make mistakes and be wrong along the way. Leaders have to move forward boldly yet be prepared, when the evidence says so, to shift course. As Fullan also said, "Learning is the work."

Educators have a rare privilege, and that is to go to work each day with the opportunity to change someone's life for the better. Many thousands of educators make that difference all the time for huge numbers of children around the world. If we are systematic about it, we can do so more often for even more young people. We must all say "yes" to that opportunity.

References

Abbott, A. (1988). *The system of professions.* Chicago, IL: University of Chicago Press.

Allensworth, E., & Easton, J. (2007). *What matters for staying on-track and graduating in Chicago public high schools.* Chicago, IL: Consortium on Chicago School Research.

Alliance for Excellent Education. (2010). *Bipartisan national public opinion poll on the need for immediate education reform.* Retrieved from http://www.all4ed.org/publication_material/July2010Poll

American Institutes for Research and SRI International. (2006). *Evaluation of the Bill & Melinda Gates Foundation's high school grants, 2001–2005.* Washington, DC: Author.

Asia Society. (2011). *Improving teacher quality around the world.* New York, NY: Author. Retrieved from http://asiasociety.org/files/lwtw-teachersummitreport0611.pdf

Balfanz, R., Bridgeland, J., Moore, L., & Fox, J. (2010). *Building a grad nation: Progress and challenge in ending the high school dropout epidemic.* Baltimore, MD: Johns Hopkins University, Everyone Graduates Center. Retrieved from http://www.americaspromise.org/Our-Work/Grad-Nation/Building-a-Grad-Nation.aspx

Barber, M., Moffit, A., & Kihn, P. (2011). *Deliverology 101: A field guide for educational leaders.* Thousand Oaks, CA: Corwin.

Barton, P. (2005). *Rising dropout rates and declining opportunities.* Princeton, NJ: Education Testing Service.

Bridgeland, J. M., Dilulio, J. J., & Morison, K. B. (2006, March). *The silent epidemic: Perspectives of high school dropouts.* Washington, DC: Civic Enterprises, LLC, in association with Peter D. Hart Research Associates for the Bill & Melinda Gates Foundation.

Bryk, A. S., Sebring, P. B., Allensworth, E., Luppescu, S., & Easton, J. Q. (2010). *Organizing schools for improvement: Lessons from Chicago.* Chicago, IL: University of Chicago Press.

Cambridge, D. (2010). *E-portfolios for lifelong learning and assessment.* San Francisco, CA: Jossey-Bass.

Campaign for Fiscal Equity. (2010). *Diploma dilemma: Rising standards, the regents diploma and schools that beat the odds.* Retrieved from http://www.overcrowdednycschools.org/downloads/Diploma_Dilemma_CFE_Report_.pdf

Canadian Council on Learning. (2008). *Evaluation of the Ontario ministry of education's student success/learning to 18 strategy* (Final report). Retrieved from http://www.edu.gov.on.ca/eng/teachers/studentsuccess/CCL_SSE_Report.pdf

Canadian Education Association. (2009). *What did you do in school today? Transforming classrooms through social, academic and intellectual engagement.* Retrieved from http://www.cea-ace.ca/sites/default/files/cea-2009-wdydist.pdf

City, E. A., Elmore, R. F., Fiarman, S. E., & Teitel, L. (2009). *Instructional rounds in education.* Cambridge, MA: Harvard Education Press.

Coleman, P. (1998). *Parent, student, and teacher collaboration: The power of three.* London, England: Paul Chapman.

Collins, J. (2001). *Good to great.* New York, NY: HarperCollins.

Csíkszentmihályi, M. (1990). *Flow: The psychology of optimal experience.* New York, NY: Harper & Row.

Cuban, L. (2001). *Oversold and underused: Computers in the classroom.* Cambridge, MA: Harvard University Press.

Cushman, K. (2010). *Fires in the mind: What kids can tell us about motivation and mastery.* San Francisco, CA: Jossey-Bass.

Darling-Hammond, L. (2010). *The flat world and education.* New York, NY: Teachers College Press.

Dillon, S. (2010, September 28). 4,100 students prove "small is better" rule wrong. *New York Times,* p. A1.

DuFour, R., DuFour, R., Eaker, B., & Many, T. (2006). *Learning by doing: A handbook for professional learning communities at work.* Bloomington, IN: Solution Tree.

Dweck, C. (2007). *Mindset: The new psychology of success.* New York, NY: Ballantine Books.

Earl, L., Torrance, N., & Sutherland, S. (2006). Changing secondary schools is hard: Lessons from 10 years of school improvement in the Manitoba School Improvement Program. In A. Harris & J. Chrispeels (Eds.), *Improving schools and educational systems* (pp. 109–128). London, England: Routledge.

Education Trust. (2008). *Core problems: Out-of-field teaching persists in key academic courses and high-poverty schools.* Retrieved from http://www.edtrust.org/issues/pre-k-12/funding-fairness

Elmore, R. F. (2004). *School reform from the inside out: Policy, practice, and performance.* Cambridge, MA: Harvard University Press.

Elmore, R. F. (2011, May 17). What would happen if we let them go? [Web log post]. Retrieved from http://blogs.edweek.org/edweek/futures_of_reform/2011/05/what_would_happen_if_we_let_them_go.html

Ferguson, B., Tilleczek, K., Boydell, K., & Rummens, J. (2005). *Early school leavers: Understanding the lived reality of student disengagement from secondary school* (Report from the Hospital for Sick Children). Retrieved from http://www.edu.gov.on.ca/eng/parents/schoolleavers.pdf

Fullan, M. (2006, November). Leading professional learning. *The School Administrator,* 10–14.

Fullan, M. (2007). *The new meaning of educational change* (3rd ed.). New York, NY: Teachers College Press.

Fullan, M. (2008). *The six secrets of change: What the best leaders do to help their organizations survive and thrive.* San Francisco, CA: Jossey-Bass.

Fullan, M. (2010a). *All systems go.* Thousand Oaks, CA: Corwin.

Fullan, M. (2010b). *Motion leadership.* Thousand Oaks, CA: Corwin.

Fullan, M. (2011). *Choosing the wrong drivers for whole system reform.* Melbourne, Australia: Centre for Strategic Education.

Gamoran, A. (2009). *Tracking and inequality: New directions for research and practice* (Working paper 2009–6). Madison: University of Wisconsin, Wisconsin Center for Education Research.

Gleason, P., & Dynarski, M. (2002). Do we know whom to serve? Issues in using risk factors to identify dropouts. *Journal of Education for Students Placed at Risk, 7*(1), 25–41.

Gregory, A., & Weinstein, R. S. (2008). The discipline gap and African Americans: Defiance or cooperation in the high school classroom. *Journal of School Psychology, 46*(4), 455–475.

Grubb, N. W. (2009). *The money myth: School resources, outcomes, and equity.* New York, NY: Russell Sage.

Grubb, N. W. (2011). *Leadership challenges in high schools: Multiple pathways to success.* Boulder, CO: Paradigm.

Hammond, C., Linton, D., Smink, J., & Drew, S. (2007). *Dropout risk factors and exemplary programs.* Clemson, SC: National Dropout Prevention Center/Communities in Schools.

Hanushek, E., & Wossman, L. (2007). *Education quality and economic growth.* Washington, DC: World Bank.

Hargreaves, A., & Fink, D. (2006). *Sustainable leadership.* San Francisco, CA: Jossey-Bass.

Harr, J., Parrish, T., Socias, M., & Gubbins, P. (2007). *Evaluation study of California's high priority school grant program* (Final report). Palo Alto, CA: American Institutes for Research.

Harris, A., & Goodall, J. (2008). Do parents know they matter? Engaging all parents in learning. *Educational Research, 50*(3), 277–289.

Harris, A., & Jones, M. (2010). Professional learning communities and system improvement. *Improving Schools, 13*(2), 172–181.

Harris Learning Commission. (2011). About the commission [Website]. Retrieved from http://www.harrisfederation.org .uk/124/about-the-commission

Harris Stefanakis, E. (2010). *Differentiated assessment: How to assess the learning potential of every student.* San Francisco, CA: Jossey-Bass.

Harvard Graduate School of Education. (2010). *The achievement gap initiative at Harvard University.* Retrieved from http://www .agi.harvard.edu/

Hattie, J. A. C. (2008). *Visible learning: A synthesis of meta-analyses relating to achievement.* London: Routledge.

Henderson, A. T., Mapp, K. L., Johnson, V. R., & Davies, D. (2007). *Beyond the bake sale: The essential guide to family-school partnerships.* New York, NY: New Press.

Herndon, J. (1971). *How to survive in your native land.* New York, NY: Simon & Schuster.

Hoffman, N. (2005). *Add and subtract: Dual enrollment as a state strategy to increase postsecondary success for underrepresented students.* Boston, MA: Jobs for the Future. Retrieved from http://www.jff.org/publications/education/add-andsubtract-dual-enrollment-state-s/156

Janosz, M. and the School Environment Research Group. (2010). *Proceeding further, together. Evaluation of New Approaches, New Solutions intervention strategy.* GRES, Universite de Montreal. Retrieved from http://www.gres-umontreal.ca/pg/siaa/siaa-rapports_sommaire-synthese.html

Jeynes, W. H. (2010, March). The salience of the subtle aspects of parental involvement and encouraging that involvement: Implications for school-based programs. *Teachers College Record, 112*(3), 747–774.

Johnson, S. M. (2004). *Finders and keepers: Helping new teachers survive and thrive in our schools.* San Francisco, CA: Jossey-Bass.

Kania, J., & Kramer, M. (2011). Collective impact. *Stanford social innovation review.* Retrieved from http://www.ssireview.org

Karoly, L., Kilburn, R., & Cannon, J. (2005). *Early childhood interventions: Proven results, future promise.* Santa Monica, CA: RAND.

Lamb, S. (2011). Pathways to school completion: An international comparison. In S. Lamb, E. Markussen, R. Teese, N. Sandberg, & J. Polesl (Eds.), *School dropout and completion* (pp. 21–73). Dordrecht, The Netherlands: Springer.

Lamb, S., Markussen, E., Teese, R., Sandberg, N., & Polesl, J. (Eds.). (2011). *School dropout and completion.* Dordrecht, The Netherlands: Springer.

Leithwood, K., & Jantzi, D. (2009). A review of empirical evidence about school size effects: A policy perspective. *Review of Educational Research, 79*(1), 464–490.

Levin, B. (2008). *How to change 5000 Schools.* Cambridge, MA: Harvard Education Press.

Levin, B. (2009). How many minutes to change a life? *Phi Kappan, 90*(5), 384–385.

Levin, B. (2010). Leadership for evidence-informed education. *School Leadership and Management, 30*(4), 303–315.

Levin, H. (2009). The economic payoff to investing in social justice. *Educational Researcher, 38*(1), 5–20.

Lightfoot, S. (1978). *Worlds apart: Relationships between families and schools.* New York, NY: Basic Books.

Lipsey, M. (2009). The primary factors that characterize effective interventions with juvenile offenders: A meta-analytic overview. *Victims and Offenders, 2*(4), 124–147.

Livingstone, D. W. (2003). *The education-jobs gap* (2nd ed.). Toronto, Canada: University of Toronto Press, Higher Education Division.

Mac Iver, D. J., & Mac Iver, M. A. (2009). *Beyond the indicators: An integrated school-level approach to dropout prevention.* Arlington, VA: The George Washington University Center for Equity and Excellence in Education.

McKinsey & Company. (2009). *The economic impact of the achievement gap in America's schools.* Washington, DC: Author.

McLaughlin, M., Atukpawu, G., & Williamson, D. and the John W. Gardner Center for Youth and Their Communities/Stanford University. (2008, March). *Alternative education options in California: A view from countries and districts.* Retrieved from http://gardnercenter.stanford.edu/docs/FINAL_AE_%20 Systems_%20Paper_%202–19–08.pdf

Muijs, D., Harris, A., Chapman, C., Stoll, L., & Russ, J. (2004). Improving schools in socio-economically disadvantaged areas: A review of the research evidence. *School Effectiveness and School Improvement, 15*(2), 149–175.

Nadirova, A., & Burger, J. (2009, April). *Improving high school completion: Using school-based accountability data to inform educational research and policies.* Paper presented to the American Educational Research Association, San Diego, CA.

National Center for Education Statistics. (2005). *Dual enrollment of high school students at postsecondary institutions: 2002–03.* Washington, DC: U.S. Department of Education. Retrieved from http://nces.ed.gov/pubs2005/2005008.pdf

National High School Center. (2007). *Findings from early college high school initiative: A look at best practices and lessons learned regarding a dual enrolment program.* Washington, DC: Author. Retrieved from http://www.betterhighschools.com/pubs/documents/NHSC_EarlyCollegeHighSchool_032107.pdf

National Research Council Institute of Medicine. (2003). *Engaging schools: Fostering high school students' motivation to learn.* Washington, DC: National Academies Press.

Newmann, F., Secada, W., & Wehlage, G. (1995). *A guide to authentic instruction and assessment: Vision, standards, and scoring.* Madison: Wisconsin Center for Education Research.

Oakes, J. (2005). *Keeping track: How schools structure inequality* (2nd ed.). New Haven, CT: Yale University Press.

Oakes, J., Renee, M., Rogers, J., & Lipton, M. (2008). Research and community organizing as tools for democratizing educational policy. In C. Sugrue (Ed.), *The future of educational change: International perspectives* (pp. 136–154). London, England: Routledge.

Organisation for Economic Co-operation and Development. (2009). *Education at a glance: 2009.* Paris, France: Author.

Organisation for Economic Co-operation and Development. (2010a). *Learning for jobs.* Paris, France: Author.

Organisation for Economic Co-operation and Development. (2010b). *PISA 2009 results: What students know and can do—student performance in reading, mathematics, and science.* (Vol. 1). Retrieved from http://browse.oecdbookshop.org/oecd/pdfs/free/9810071e.pdf

Organisation for Economic Co-operation and Development. (2011). *Building a high quality teaching profession: Lessons from around the world.* Paris, France: Author.

Organisation for Economic Co-operation and Development and Statistics Canada. (2010). *Pathways to success: How knowledge and skills at age 15 shape future lives in Canada.* Ottawa: Author.

Ou, S. (2008). Do GED recipients differ from graduates and school dropouts? Findings from an inner-city cohort. *Urban Education, 43*(1), 83–117.

Pekrul, S., & Levin, B. (2007). Building student voice for school improvement. In D. Thiessen & A. Cook-Sather (Eds.), *International handbook of student experience in elementary and secondary school* (pp. 711–726). Dordrecht, The Netherlands: Springer.

Pushor, D. (2010). Are schools doing enough to learn about families? In M. Miller Marsh & T. Turner-Vorbeck (Eds.). *(Mis) understanding families: Learning from real families in our schools* (pp. 4–16). New York, NY: Teachers College Press.

Reeves, D. B. (2010). *Transforming professional development into student results.* Alexandria, VA: ASCD.

Rothstein, R. (2004). *Class and schools: Using social, economic, and educational reform to close the black-white achievement gap.* Washington, DC: Economic Policy Institute.

Rumberger, R. (2011). High school dropouts in the United States. In S. Lamb, E. Markussen, R. Teese, N. Sandberg, & J. Polesl

(Eds.), *School dropout and completion* (pp. 275–294). Dordrecht, The Netherlands: Springer.

Rumberger, R. W., & Lim, S. A. (2008). *Why students drop out of school: A review of 25 years of research.* Santa Barbara: California Dropout Research Project.

Shirley, D. (2008). Community organizing for educational change: Past illusions, future prospects. In C. Sugrue (Ed.), *The future of educational change* (pp. 89–105). New York, NY: Routledge.

Singleton, G., & Linton, C. (2005). *Courageous conversations about race: Field guide for achieving equity in schools.* Thousand Oaks, CA: Sage.

Smith, R., & Lambert, M. (2008). Assuming the best. *Educational Leadership, 66*(1), 16–21.

Society for Research in Child Development. (2010). School-based mentoring: Weighing future investments. *Sharing youth and child development knowledge, 24*(3). Retrieved from http://www.srcd.org/index.php?option=com_content&task=view&id=229&Itemid=551.

Stanovich, K. (2005). *The robot's rebellion.* Chicago, IL: University of Chicago Press.

Summit told U.S. high schools 'obsolete.' (2005, February 26). *Associated Press.* Retrieved from http://www.msnbc.msn.com/id/7033821/ns/us_news-education/t/summit-told-us-high-schools-obsolete/#.Tmzdp-zwOSo

Swanson, C. (2011). Analysis finds graduation rates moving up. *Education Week, 30*(34), 23–25. Retrieved from http://tinyurl.com/6bfm7tk

Tamim, R., Bernard, R. M., Borokhovski, E., Abrami, P. C., & Schmid, R. F. (2011). What forty years of research says about the impact of technology on learning: A second-order meta-analysis and validation study. *Review of Educational Research, 81*(1), 14–28.

Tavris, C., & Aronson, E. (2008). *Mistakes were made . . . but not by me.* Boston, MA: Houghton Mifflin.

Teese, R. (2011). Vocational education and training in France and Germany. In S. Lamb, E. Markussen, R. Teese, N. Sandberg, & J. Polesl (Eds.), *School dropout and completion* (pp. 343–356). Dordrecht, The Netherlands: Springer.

Thiessen, D., & Cook-Sather, A. (Eds.). (2007). *International handbook of student experience in elementary and secondary school.* Dordrecht, The Netherlands: Springer.

Timperley, H., Wilson, A., Barrar, H., & Fung, I. (2007). *Teacher professional learning and development.* Wellington, New Zealand: Best Evidence Synthesis (BES) Iteration, Ministry of Education.

U.S. Department of Education. (2011). *International summit on the teaching profession.* Retrieved from http://www2.ed.gov/about/inits/ed/internationaled/teaching-summit.html

Wagner, T. (2008). *The global achievement gap.* New York, NY: Basic Books.

Webb, M., & Mayka, L. (2010). *Unconventional wisdom: A profile of the graduates of early college high school.* Boston, MA: Jobs for the Future. Available at http://www.jff.org

Whitaker, C. (2011). *The impact of dual credit on college access and participation: An Ontario case study* (Unpublished EdD dissertation). University of Toronto, Canada.

William, D. (2008). Changing classroom practice. *Educational Leadership, 65*(4), 36–42.

Wlodkowski, R. J. (1983). *Motivational opportunities for successful teaching.* [Leader's guide]. Phoenix, AZ: Universal Dimensions.

World Bank. (2005). *Expanding opportunities and building competencies: A new agenda for secondary education.* Washington, DC: Author.

Index

CORWIN
A SAGE Company

The Corwin logo—a raven striding across an open book—represents the union of courage and learning. Corwin is committed to improving education for all learners by publishing books and other professional development resources for those serving the field of PreK–12 education. By providing practical, hands-on materials, Corwin continues to carry out the promise of its motto: **"Helping Educators Do Their Work Better."**

ONTARIO PRINCIPALS' COUNCIL
Exemplary Leadership in Public Education

The Ontario Principals' Council (OPC) is a voluntary association for principals and vice-principals in Ontario's public school system. We believe that exemplary leadership results in outstanding schools and improved student achievement. To this end, we foster quality leadership through world-class professional services and supports. As an ISO 9001 registered organization, we are committed to **"quality leadership—our principal product."**